COLORED SEATED IN THE REAR

NANCY LEE MCCASKILL
with contributions by
Adeline Reddick

QUAILS' NEST PUBLISHING

MURRELLS INLET, SC

Cover by Berge Design

ISBN-13: 978-0-986-4005-5-1

DEDICATION

Adeline and I dedicate this book to all children of the Sixties of the South, especially sons and daughters of farmers, farm hands and sharecroppers. We all are a special breed and have a such special bond. As they say, "You just would have had to have been there!"

CONTENTS

SPECIAL THANKS
to our sponsors and friends who supported us
both financially and with encouragement

Dawn F. Ellen
Bruce McCathren
Jewell Bounds
Betty Manning Heriot
Jenni Palm
Rebekah J. Murphy
Linda Spodick
Lindy Bramlett
Karen R. McPherson
Susan Josey Smith
Tammy Zoerhof
Evie G. Robertson
Janice K. Kahaly
Michael Farver
Wanda F. Gerasimek
Lena McCutchen
Natalie Silva
Lori Uloa
Ara Boyer
Stacy Masters
Anne C. Pittard
Rosalie Hyatt
Steve Cohoon
Karla Parriott

Jerry Fox Law
Rebecca Creighton
Holly Jackson
Linda S. Baker
Pat Barletta
Jeanette Bodie
Junior Hopkins
Richard Wotruba
Patti Talles
Elaine K. Dickinson
Edna Tisdale
Gloria Allen
Tandra Alderman
Colleen H. Graham
Linda Jordan
Elizabeth Baynard
Tami Devour
Jan C. Bailey
Gloria Stewart
Amy C. Barlow
Charlene H. Privette
Tracy Holscher
Teresa Gecevich
Pat Peele

Rosemary Carter
Sharren McGarry
Bobo Moore
Vicki Himmelman
Jeannie Mazza
Pat Maldonado
Sarah Stokes Steadman
Cindy Fanney
Julie Powers
Michelle S. Bass
Debbie D. Meyer
Kami B. McMahan
Marissa Frederick
Tracy Graham
Jean Broadway
Rhonda Spradley
Sharon Holland
Audrey Hoover
Renee A. Clark
Young Jamie Vernon
Bobbie Boyce
Michael D. Vernon
Kathy Bregar

Linda J. Connell
Laura Bennett
Liz Simon
Fran Crolley
Moye S. Harrison
Amy Boyd
Pam Clemmons
Cindy Howland
Dale Geddings
Michael Pressley
Kathryn Welch
Jettie Mescher
Marjorie Townsend
Kim Martier
Mark Payne
JoFrieda Kelly
Judy B. Alderman
Sarah Card
Tammy Ware
Ben Gay III
Etha Bailey
Bob Samara
Kathy G. Oakley

Melonie and Keith Griffin

PROLOGUE

"You never really understand a person until you consider things from his point of view...until you climb inside his skin and walkaround in it."

To Kill a Mockingbird-Harper Lee

I became keenly aware of white privilege as a white child at the age of five, although I did not have a name for it then or begin to understand its effect on our society until five decades later. On the other hand, my black playmate, Adeline, knew and expressed what it meant from the day she could talk. Adeline had a unique way of making sure I was aware of my privilege and, at the same time, making me aware she put her panties on the same way I did. She still does!

Adeline and I grew up on the same farm in the 1950's and '60's in Lee County, South Carolina. We were friends as little girls on the farm, but she was a bit older than I. In writing this story, we adjusted the timeline so that the two little girls were closer in age. The characters in this story are compilations of people and events and our different experiences then that shaped our perspectives on how our country has gotten to where we are now. For me, it is mostly a memoir of life growing up on the farm, although parts of the story are completely made up. At times Adeline and I couldn't remember exactly the way things really happened, or we knew others that had similar experiences in the 60s. For Adeline, the story is an account reliving repression, the nightmare of Negro life in the South during her childhood.

5

For me, our discussions while writing were eye-opening; for Adeline, they were painful, and it was painful to watch her relive. We both debated about whether certain family embarrassing moments should be included. The litmus test was 1) is this something that happened to a lot of us in the sixties, and 2) was it really a family secret or did the family just try to keep it secret, but everyone knew anyway? As result, not much was left out and we realize much of it will be controversial. Isn't that what makes for a juicy book, after all? Just know that we both love our families very much, forgave everybody long ago, and we now know much worse things happened to other children.

Adeline and I both moved away from South Carolina for better opportunities and lost touch. Then one day I called the Lee County Library in Bishopville, SC, and asked to speak to the librarian. Dawn Ellen was a high school friend of mine, and she knew everyone in town. I asked if she knew any black women that frequented the library that may have grown up near Lyndale Farms, the McCaskill farm in the Turkey Creek-St. Matthews area of Lee County. I knew it was a long shot, but I wanted to see if someone would be interested in writing a book with me from the perspective of a little Black girl growing up on a farm in the sixties. Imagine my surprise when she laughed and said, "Well, how about Adeline Reddick? She works here."

I felt as though I had won the lottery! Adeline and I reconnected, and our friendship grew. The more we talked about the things that made us different, the more we learned how much we were and are alike. She was the perfect choice for a co-author, not only because our families had been so closely intertwined, but because she was enthusiastic about reconnecting and the project, too. The character named Sunshine, or Shine, is loosely shaped by Adeline's recollections and feelings. The McDonald family in the story is similar my family.

Adeline now lives on Reddick Road, a street named after her father, in a subdivision on land she bought from my father. He cleared some of the woods on timber land he owned and sold lots to many of the black people that had worked for our family when HUD houses were first built. I inherited all the unsold land and timber left in that subdivision. Adeline now helps me sell the few lots that remain.

One day Adeline and I were riding around the roads in her subdivision looking at the different empty lots and came across someone's property that had trash all over it. Adeline said that a trailer had caught on fire and exploded. The owner never cleared the trash. He had built a tacky, one-room shack on the property in the meantime. The mess made the whole neighborhood look bad. We were going on and on about it, and when I asked Adeline if I should talk to him, she said hastily, "It ain't gonna do no good, he ain't nothing but white trash!"

Adeline clamped her hands over her mouth, looked at me wide-eyed, and held her breath. I burst out laughing and she finally did, too.

"I forgot you're white!"

We laughed and laughed, and at that moment, I knew we no longer saw each other's skin color. However, since we both identified this man as "white trash," we knew we still had some discrimination issues. Both of us are works in progress, as is our nation. Please be patient.

Colored Seated in the Rear

CHAPTER ONE
~ *Lee~5 yrs. Old (1961)*

*"When I was younger, I could remember anything,
whether it had happened or not; but my faculties are
decaying now and soon it shall be so I cannot remember
any but the things that never happened. It is sad to go to
pieces like this, but we all have to do it."*

Mark Twain

In 1961, Ernest Hemingway, Ty Cobb, and my baby brother, Roger Stokes McDonald died. The only one that mattered to me, or my parents or brother and sister, was that sweet blue-eyed, dimpled cherub with a hole in his heart that left a gaping hole in ours. Roger's hair was so blonde it was white and his eyes so blue they looked like two little ponds of tears most of the time. His lips and fingernails were blue from lack of oxygen and were a constant reminder of his condition. For me, at five, he was my living baby doll. However, he was a living nightmare for my parents who knew they had a beautiful baby who would probably never live long enough to have heart surgery. When he died in November of 1961 at only sixteen months-old, my mother went into a deep depression. After that, I always wanted to "do it myself" rather than have to ask Mama for anything and tried to mother my siblings so Mama could "rest." As the days warmed from spring into summer the following year, I took my three-year old sister outside to play with me more and my dad took my four-year old brother to the farm with him more. We did not want them to hear her crying so much or my siblings incessantly asking, "When is Little Roger coming home?"

One of the things I could not do by myself was tie my shoes. We didn't have Velcro back then. Mama tried to teach me to tie them, but I could not see the darn bunny ears. "Make a bunny ear with this lace and wrap the other one around it," she would say. I had a spectacular imagination when it came to my own thoughts and creations, but I took everyone else quite literally. If Mama was going to talk about a bunny rabbit, I expected to see it with my own eyes! I went around barefooted or with my shoelaces untied most of the time, on the lookout for bunnies. I was fascinated with them to the point that every birthday cake and gift had bunnies on them. I even hunted for them in the woods, thinking I needed to really examine those ears closely to see how they related to tying my shoes!

I loved going to the woods behind our house. I was six and Pam was about to turn four when we found a clearing in the woods behind our house. The middle area was covered in a patchy but lush carpet of moss in the middle of sandy soil like an oasis in a desert. It was probably eight to ten feet in diameter. Small pine and oak trees stood sparsely around the edges in the sand. We imagined the thick green moss in the woods was our carpet for a house my sister and I along with friends spent the summer decorating our special place.

Pam and I found all sorts of things in the woods people had dumped because back then people burned trash or hauled what could not be burned to the woods. There was no trash pick-up. We drug a stained and tattered, yellow couch with no legs to the corner of the moss carpet, put an old pot-bellied stove in our kitchen, and made a table out of a piece of weathered, slightly warped plywood. We used old buckets and stumps for stools, and plates and bottles were easy to come by. As the summer dragged on, we added more and more finds to our outdoor play area.

We went to the woods almost daily that summer. The playhouse was a great distraction from my mother's sadness and my father's anger that always seemed directed at me. Pam had an invisible playmate, Cherry, who almost always tagged along. I had some Black playmates from the farm I usually invited, or they just showed up: my favorite playmate the head sharecropper's daughter, Adeline, who we called Shine, or some shy children across the road, Puddin, Moonpie, and Knee-Boy. I always liked the name Knee-Boy—they said it meant he was the second baby from the last and came to his mammie's knee. I think he was around three, but he was still in diapers and did not talk, only grunted and pointed. Moonpie was my age. I am guessing her nickname was from her perfectly round, face. Her sister, Puddin was tall and lanky and a little older than us. All of them had blue-black skin and had bulging bellies with skinny little legs. I realize now it was probably from malnourishment, although Shine, who also visited occasionally, convinced me they had worms. Maybe it was, but they definitely were underfed children. Shine was always neat and clean, but the others were barely dressed, dirty, and always had dried, yellow snot smeared across their little faces. They would wipe their noses with the back of their hands. My little sister would stare at them and then glare at me. She knew I would never let her get away with that! I didn't say anything because I knew they did not know any better. Their clothes were too little for them and did not cover their big bellies. Knee-Boy wore only diapers; and none of them ever wore shoes, even in the woods. We were not allowed to go in the woods without our shoes, no bare feet, or flip flops. Of course, most of the time, my shoelaces were not tied unless Shine showed up.

Pam and I had not had the playhouse quite a month when one day, we were walking down the path toward the playhouse behind our house, singing, "Row, Row, Row your

Boat," and much to our delight we could hear Puddin and Moonpie coming from a side road, singing it, too! When we both reached the playhouse, I taught them how to counterpoint their singing over our singing like our mother taught us. We were giggling, making hand motions, and spinning, singing "Row, row, row your boat; life is but a dream. Merrily, merrily, merrily, gently down the stream!"

Out of the corner of my eye, I saw someone coming down the path opposite from the way Pam and I came into the woods. Instinctively, I huddled everyone together, startled.

It was Shine!

"Shine! How did you know how to get to my house the back way!" I said, and we all relaxed.

"I didn't. I jes heared y'all singing, and I followed it from the cornfield."

"What are you doing in the cornfield?" Puddin asked,

"My mama is picking corn over at the Kelly's, and I was hoeing weeds." She thumped her hoe on the ground.

"She makes you work on a Saturday?" I asked.

"Sat-day, Monday, ever day, chile," she sighed.

"Well, play with us a while before you go back!" I grinned, and Shine grinned back. "We are about to make breakfast on our stove." I pointed like a TV model to our elegant living area.   Moonpie made a dash for the stove. "Well, that's good cuz I sho' is hungry! I found this old coffee pot last time we was here," she said.

Puddin sat down on a stump and patted one for Shine. "Come sit down. These gonna be our coffee mugs and milk glasses." And with that, she tapped the old beer bottles on the table.

Pam had picked some wildflowers and stuck them in an empty Crown Royal bottle in the center of the table and pointed at an empty Miller beer bottle. "Miller!" she said.

"Oh lawd!" Shine exclaimed, "Don't tell me that baby can read? How she knowed what that say? "

"TV," I said.

"Y'all got a TV?" Moonpie asked as she pretend-poured our coffee.

"Yep, don't you?" thinking in my six-year-old head everyone in the world had one.

"Naw" said all three Black girls at once.,

"Oh," immediately feeling horrible I had asked. "Oh my! We forgot our food! Everyone, go gather something to bring to the table to pretend-eat."

When we sat back down to our "coffee," we had juniper berries, leaves for toast, rocks for eggs, and cockleburs. Pam and Knee-Boy took their finds to the couch as we only had seating for four at the table. We were going on and on about how good our feast was. Knee-Boy got curious. He wandered over to the table and tried to really eat the juniper berries and cockleburs. I slapped them out of his hands.

"No, Knee-Boy, you can't really eat those! They will hurt you, baby!"

Pam came over and gave me a dirty look and patted him on the back.

"It's ok. You can come eat with me and Cherry," she said haughtily as she grabbed his hand, then walked behind him, pushing him back toward the couch. He was bow-legged and waddled as he walked, and she had started walking like him. She mimicked everybody.

We were laughing so hard; but when they got to the couch, the little resourceful girl had green plums and sour grass collected on a nest of pine straw and was offering him real food! I was amazed. We only had fake food.

"All of that's ok to eat, but don't eat the pine straw!" I advised.

Shine was sniffing in the air, looking at the other two Black girls. "Oh, my Lord. Y'all niggers stink!" Shine blurted out, holding her nose.

"Shine!" I fussed at her, surprised.

"Well, they do! Don't y'all ever bathe?" She said with a disgusted look on her face.

Puddin and Moonpie just glared at her. They did have a strong odor, but I wasn't going to say anything, Heck, my daddy smelled like cow manure every night when he came in from the farm. My mother dared us to say anything about it, or you wouldn't be able to walk for a week.

Shine persisted, "Don't y'all have a hand pump so you can bathe? "

Puddin and Moonpie hung their heads and continued glaring at us. Knee-Boy sat down at his sisters' feet and proceeded to pick his nose.

Shine lowered her voice and looked at me, "Well, I guess you McDonalds have running water?" She said it more like a proud, elegant statement than a taunting question.

"What's 'running' water?" Moonpie asked innocently.

For a split second, I pictured water with legs, running down the road and chuckled. I quickly suppressed it because I surely did not want her to think I was laughing at her.

Shine explained that they got water out of a pump that you had to prime whereas the McDonalds and most white folks just turned on the spicket and hot or cold water would come out, whatever you wanted. Good Lord, I was so thankful for that, at the time; but now I know so many other things I am even more grateful for now, thanks to Shine.

"Shine, we do have a well outside and we can just get hot or cold any time, even in the bathtub. But how do you take a bath using a hand pump?

"Well, dear heart, you knowed that your granddaddy, Mr. Alvie, had a hand pump outside his back door, right? And you just put a little water in it to it to prime it, and then you pumps the handle, right?"

I nodded. I was always fascinated with it.

"And you get a bucket and put under it, and you pump and pump. Then you heat the water on the pot-bellied stove like this one," and she points to the dilapidated contraption in our playhouse. "You McDonalds probably have a 'lectric stove, right?"

I nodded, trying not to look too proud, but all I could think of was all the things she would have to do to get hot water: find wood, chop it, burn it in the stove...I would just settle for stinking, too!

Shine stood up and moved back away from us a bit as if she could no longer take the stench. She used her hands as she talked. "We divides the hot water into two wash tubs in two rooms,
one for the mens and one for the girls." She walks through our moss carpet like she is dividing the house.

I watched the girls to see if they were listening. Moonpie dug her toes in the ground and started rolling her tongue in her cheek. Puddin put her hand on her hip with her head cocked toward Shine as if this were the first time she had ever heard how to prepare for a bath.

"The mens goes to one room to bathe and the girls to the other for more privacy. Ooh, don't you know it feel so good to get all that ashiness off!" Shine said, brushing her arms.

Puddin looked uncomfortable and started rubbing her arms, too. You could see flecks of dead skin flying off her in the sunlight.

Shine came over and half-whispered to me, "We ought to hose them down."

"Aw, Shine", I said, "Go pretend-eat your breakfast."

"Do your mama's hose reach this far?"

"No!" said Pam.

"She knows, "I laughed, "She's already tried to drag it out here to make mudpies."

"Ain't nothing better than cold water from a hose," Moonpie said, and we all agreed, but then we knew she had heard us.

All of the sudden, Shine said that she heard her mother yelling for her from the cornfield and reached for her hoe.

About the same time, I saw my little sister crouched down in her green polka dot sundress and I headed for her. I thought she was pooping in her pants. She was potty-trained, but she'd had a few mishaps since little Roger died, partly because I was her main caretaker and could not remember to remind her to "go."

"Pretty worm!" she said, pointing for me to see.

I don't know who moved faster, me, Shine, or the stinky girls. I grabbed my sister, Shine leaped across the carpet and was beside me in a flash with her hoe, and the other girls went flying in the opposite direction, yelling, "Snake!!" Shine used her expert hoeing skills on the head of one of the biggest snakes I had ever seen in my six years of life and killed that ugly, skanky reptile.

"Lawd Jesus! Lawd Jesus! Help us, Lawd Jesus!" Puddin and Moonpie were standing a good distance away, their scrawny legs quivering, pleading with Jesus as if that snake would eat us all! They left Knee-Boy in the middle of the moss carpet, clapping his hands at the antics, happily laughing at us, with more snot running down his nose into his mouth.

I was too young to know if the snake was poisonous or not, and Shine said she didn't care if it was or not, she hated snakes, and it needed to be "kilt." Shine was brave and was my hero from that day forward! Snakes and other critters from the nearby swamp never stopped me from playing in the woods. It apparently never bothered my mother and father much, but my father did go out and remove the dead snake. Afterwards he put sulfur in a big perimeter of the play area to keep the snakes away. I never remember seeing another one there, although I saw plenty more in my childhood.

In another couple of days, Pam and I were playing in the woods again as if it never happened. For Moonpie and Puddin, however, it took a little longer.

CHAPTER TWO

—Adeline—Summer of 1962

*"I'd like to teach the world to sing in perfect harmony.
I'd like to hold it in my arms and keep it company."*

Billy Davis

I got to the McDonald girls' playhouse before the other girls did one day. I knowed they all gonna be there because we was going celebrate something. Turns out, Pam and Moonpie had the same birthday! That's right, June 15th. I wanted to get there early so I could decorate. I painted pinecones pink with some old paint I found in the woods and strung them from tree to tree with some old tobacco twine. I couldn't wait to give them the little presents I made for them. I got Moonpie a doll I had made out of a shucked ear of corn, and I braided the silks hanging out the top. Now Pam, she being white and all, probably had a toy box full of toys, so I got to thinking what I could give her and decided on something I was sure she ain't never had: one of my mama's prized little lemon pies. Only this time, Mama let me help her make it, so it was real special. I liked cooking a daggum lot more than I liked working in the field. And I liked giving. My mama said I won't ever gonna have nothing because I'll be done give it all away. But least I'll be happy, and I sho will make somebody else happier than I am. That is the daggum truth.

While I was waiting on ever body and thinking about all this, I played my favorite little game to pass the time away: Doo Loo. I loved to take a piece of pine straw to a hole in the sand and sweet talk those little doodle bugs right out of the ground.

"Doodle Loo, Doo Loo, bread and butter.

Doodle Loo, Doo Loo, come to supper.

Doodle Loo, Doo Loo, your house is on fire,

Doodle Loo, Doo Loo, come out of your hole, "

When all the chilren got to the woods, they say, "Show us how to do that Shine!" By then I had three doodle bugs on my palm to show them.

"Shine, why are your hands white on that side and brown on the other," Pam innocently askt me.

Pam was turning over Moonpie's hands to see if hers were the same way. Puddin and Moonpie looked at their hands as if they had never noticed they own hands before.

"Pam! Shh!" Lee was trying to keep the poor little thing from questioning our skin color in front of us, but Lord knows I was used to it by then. Ever where you go you was reminded of it; sign, signs, ever where a sign: "colored seated to the rear", "colored restroom", "colored water fountain" or "no Blacks allowed at the soda fountain". When I was Pam's age, shoot, I thought the whites were colored. We was just brown and white. So-called white peoples was all shades of pink, sometimes spotted with freckles and had red, blonde, black or brown hair, with them green, blue, or brown eyes. Why were WE colored when they was multi-colored, and we were jes plain old brown and white? Heck, we ain't even really black. As usual, I guess I ain't got no say in the matter, but it don't seem right to me.

I laughed, "All of us have a little white *and* black in us—you probably do, too, honey chile. God put it there to remind people we is all one race. Don't forget that. He should have made the bottom of the white man's foot black, so he'd remember that when he's sticking it in his mouth."

"I thought we was here for a burfday party, not polly ticks," Puddin pouted. "Show us how to do Doo Loo."

I showed them how, and pretty shortly, all of us had doodle bugs in our hands.

"You see how they scoot backwards. They don't never go forward."

"Yeah, like Knee-Boy. He only crawlt backwards. He ain't ever crawlt forward," said Moonpie.

Puddin agreed, "Yeah, it's a wonder that bow-legged chile can walk!"

We all laughed. That Pam always laughed at ever thing. She be the happiest chile. I never knew if she understood what she was laughing at. Now that she was turning four, I was hoping she would be more of a playmate to Lee and not such a baby. Lee was really too young to be taking care of her in the woods so much, and for the life of me, I couldn't figure out why them rich people would let their chillun run loose in the woods like that. 'Specially when they had running water and 'lectric stoves. Shoot, they could hire babysitters. Maybe I should have askt Ma if I could have been their babysitter rather than worked in the fields.

"Knee-Boy ain't coming," Moonpie blurted out.

"We ain't got no washing machine, and Ma and Knee-Boy be sick," Puddin explained.

"Sorry they be sick. We ain't got a machine neither. I bet you McDonald's got one," I smiled at Lee. I didn't say it mean. I just knew when I grew up and got out of this hell-hole I was gonna have ever thing the McDonalds had, 'cept it won't gonna include no dang cotton fields.

Lee never answered me, but, of course, I knew the answer. In a bit, she asked me in a real low tone, "Well, how do you wash your clothes?"

She really didn't know.

"With a warsh board and water heated on the stove just like for our baths. Mama makes us lye soap and it will get the stain out of anything! Even poop outa baby diapers. Your grandma, Miss Eltie, gets if from my mama and says it is THE best. Uh huh. So, after you scrub them on the warsh board, you hang them out to dry on the clothesline."

Lee said, "We have a clothesline, too, but we use the dryer if it's raining, or we are burning trash in the barrel out back."

"And we use it if Lizzie is ringing chicken necks out back and signing them. It smells and it makes Lee puke," Pam done told on Lee!

"Hush. You don't have to tell everything! And it's singeing, not signing. I get sick thinking about it. Ugh!" Lee made a pukey face.

All us black girls giggled. That was the least of what would make us sick. The vision of Miss Lizzie *signing* dead chickens cracks me up to this day.

When we tired of Doo Loo I sez, "Ok, Miss Pam and Miss Moonpie, what would you like to do next for y'all's birthday?"

Lee speaks up before they can and says, "We brought a couple of buckets of water to make some mud pies. They've wanted to do that for the longest. Y'all look up at the pretty pink decorations Shine did for you! Aren't they beautiful!"

The girls all looked up and clapped and sounded like they just loved them. I was so proud I had made them happy.

"I knew y'all was gonna want to make pies so guess what I brought you? Surprise! Mama gave me some of her old little pie tins for us to play with today. "

I proudly pulled out my tins and give each girl one. We got busy digging under the sand to get to the darker dirt because it held the water better. Puddin and I got an old beer bottle and poured enough water in each girl's pie tin to make a decent pie with her sand. After we got it all mixed up, we hunted for flowers, seeds and twigs and things to decorate them with. They was not enough chairs to go around, so Lee sat Pam in the middle of the plywood table, and just as we were about to sing "Happy Birthday," Pam poured a whole bottle of water into her pie pan. After that, her four pretend-candlesticks would not stand up. Everyone except Pam scrambled from the table to fix her cake. One of us dumped the old one, one got new sand, one got four new twigs, and one got some new decorations. When we came back to the table, Miss Pam had started the party without us. She had mud all over her hands and face and a look that said, "Yuck!"

"Oh baby! Look at her, Lee. She done gone ahead and ate somebody's mud cake. God bless her little heart!" I laughed and laughed.

Everybody laughed and laughed hard, 'cept Lee. She said, "Mama is gonna have my hide."

I said, "Don't tell her."

Lee took her T-shirt off, started wiping Pam off, and said, "This little brat tells her everything and makes up more to blame me with." She made her spit the mud out of her mouth with water from one of the old beer bottles.

Sounded like my sister, um hmm.

We sang Happy Birthday to Pam and Moonpie, then I gave them my presents. Only problem was, Pam wanted the corn doll and Moonpie wanted the pie. So, I lets them switch. I guess Moonpie was starving, and I can't tell you what make a little white girl want another baby doll when she prob'ly got ten of the dang things at home. Greed, I reckon. Most all white folks is nothing but greedy.

I said, "Ok, the birthday girls get to pick out what we gonna do next."

"Sing," Moonpie said.

"Sing," Pam mimicked.

"I will go along with that," I said. I love to sing.

Lee suggested we make a stage like they do at their house around the fireplace when they sing for their family and friends. So, we moved things around on the moss carpet to give us more room and turned the cinder blocks on their sides to make a stage with the plywood. As each of us performed, the rest of us sat our behinds on that filthy couch. But we did have so much fun!

"Moonpie, you go first," Pam said.

Moonpie be a little bashful so she askt Puddin to sing with her. It didn't escape me that the colored chilllun got to go first, bless Pam's heart. Lord, those chillun might be stinky, but they sure could sing. They sang, "This Little Light of Mine." Lee and Pam joined in singing the second round. They said their mama was the children's choir director at their church, and that be one of the first songs she taught all them chilren at St. Matthews. Imagine that—them teaching those chillun black spirituals and do unto others and not let nary one black person cross the threshold of their doors! At the time, "This Little Light of Mine" was an anthem in the Civil Rights movement. I wonder if Miss Joannie knew that. Maybe she for us and not against us, I don't know, but I do know Mr. Alvie and Mrs. Eltie, their grandparents, treated my family real good. My daddy, Colin Reddick, was his head sharecropper and they really looked after each other. Mrs. Eltie said me and Mama and Peggy are the onliest ones that can ride in her car cuz we was clean. Peggy worked for her sometimes, and we was all on the farm a lot.

After that, Pam and Lee sang, "How much is that Doggie in the Window," and had the audience, which was the rest of us, say "Ruff, ruff" when she gave us the cue. Moonpie kept saying 'ruff ruff' at the wrong time and I almost peed in my pants laughing. Sometimes Lee would forget to give us the cue, and it was even funnier.

Next, Pam, with her cute little pixie haircut and perky personality sang "I'm a Little Teapot". She followed it with what Lee called "tapping." Said she was taking lessons. White peoples actually pay to have their chilren take all kinds of "lessons," ballet, piano, art. Like if you ain't born with talent, them fools think you can buy it! Ha!

I decided I wanted to teach them some songs, so I taught them "Itsy Bitsy Spider" and a couple more. We ended the party with all of us in a circle, singing "He's Got the Whole World in His Hands." We were all clapping, and the black girls had a perfect beat going. Lee seemed to be perfectly aware she was having a hard time keeping rhythm. I winked at her and smiled, "We was born with it in our blood, baby!"

Moonpie laughed, "She ain't got a lick of black blood in her!"

Puddin nodded toward Pam, "I ain't so sho about her…she got pretty good rhythm for a white gal!"

We were all getting ready to go and Pam said, "I want to sing one more!"

"Sure, it's your birthday, darling. Go right ahead. You need a microphone?" I asked and I handed her part of a tree branch that sort of looked like one.

Pam beamed and had that devilish gleam in her eye, so I knew she be up to something. She hopped up on the "stage" and made sho' we was all listening and sang, in a baby voice:

"There's just one Schlitz, yeah, yeah
    Nothing else comes near,
    When you're out of Schlitz,
    you're out of beer!
    If you like it cold with a nasty taste, too,

    There's only one brew that will do.
    When you're out of Schlitz,
    You're out of beer!
    Real gusto in a great, lite beer! Schlitz! Yeah!"

We was all in stitches! When she said Schlitz, it sounded more like "shits." Oh, my lord, we laughed and laughed.

Puddin bragged, "That's the kind of beer my daddy drinks when he be home."

I picked the Schlitz bottle off the table. "Pam, how you say this?"

"Shits," she says, convinced she was saying it correctly.

"Schlitz," I said, emphasizing the "l".

"Shits", she repeated, nodding and smiling.

"Lee, how she know all them words about beer?" I asked.

"TV," Lee said.

I thought to myself maybe it be best most of these black chilren don't have a television if that's the mess they learn. But it sho was funny.

"I best be getting back to the fields. Lee, did you bring me a rag and soap like I askt you?" I looked over at her.

"Yeah, you going to take it home with you?" Lee reached in her pocket and handed it to me.

"No, it's not for me, these sweet li'l niggas still stink. Puddin, you and Moonpie got to bathe if you are going to hang around me, and you sho got to smell good if you gonna play with Mrs. Eltie's grand chillun. Take off your shirts and use that water left in the bucket. Take turns with the soap and rag and scrub, you hear me?"

"Yessum," they both said, hanging their heads.

CHAPTER THREE

~Lee~6 yrs. old/summer of 1962

"Early childhood is like being highly intoxicated
everyone remembers what you did except you!"

Lee McDonald (to Pam)

One big part of my life and Shine's growing up was church. Back then our churches weren't integrated, so I went to St. Matthews Methodist Church a mile from my house, and Shine went to Mount Zion AME (African Methodist Episcopal) a mile from hers. My granddaddy gave us a silver dollar if we attended church all year without missing a single Sunday, so I did not miss many, even if we were out of town. Two of the highlights of summer each year was vacation bible school, followed a few weeks later by a revival. I got saved every year. I thought it would protect me from the wrath of my daddy, but it did not.

We always had a guest preacher at our revival, and my parents always invited both pastors to dinner one night during revival. I have long forgotten any of these other dinners, but the one for the summer of '62, I will never forget. Even though that night was over fifty years ago, it made a huge impression on me because of the phenomenal meal my mother made, the stupendous thing my little sister did in front of dinner guests, and the relentless spanking I got afterwards.

My mother was a great cook. To this day, I think what she made that night was the best meal I have ever tasted. It is still my favorite meal: slow-cooked roast beef with rich, brown gravy and rice, field peas, tomatoes, fried okra, stuffed squash, and buttermilk biscuits. We always had plenty of good food. We grew garden vegetables like butterbeans, peas, collards, turnips, squash and okra, and fruit like blueberries, blackberries, strawberries, melons, plums, grapes, and pears. We had our own corn, grits, flour, honey, butter, and milk. We had beef, dairy cows, pigs, chickens and we hunted quail and turkey. The only thing we ever bought at the store was bread, Duke's mayonnaise, and sugar. And once in a blue moon, Mama would get one, just one, Baby Ruth candy bar and split it four ways.

Pam and I had been in the woods as usual the day before revival started, the same day the preachers were coming to dinner. I could hear Mama calling us to come home that afternoon, but we were having too much fun making mud pies to come home. We weren't celebrating Pam's birthday officially until we could do it in between hers and my brother's because they had birthdays in the same month. I felt sorry for her not having her own party so I wanted to party in the woods with her as long as I could. To be honest, I forgot the preachers were coming!

When Pam and I heard my dad calling us, then we knew we had to leave, without question.

We ran to the house, out of breath, and walked into the dining room already seated with guests.

My mother gasped, "You have mud all over you! What on earth have you two been up to?"

Rev. Jacobs and the guest pastor smiled sympathetically and pursed their lips.

"We've been in the woods playing in the woods with the niggers!" I told them excitedly.

Everyone gasped.

"Nancy Lee! You mean little black children. We don't use that word!" My mom snapped.

My dad cleared his throat and looked at me disapprovingly.

"Well, that's what Shine called them. She said they stink, but we took care of that!" I said proudly.

My mother's mouth flew open, not knowing quite what to say. "Excuse me for a minute please," she nodded toward her guests. "Let me go and get these girls cleaned up."

She had us each by one arm, dragging us off towards the bathroom.

"Go ahead and serve yourselves; I will be right back," she said over her shoulder to her guests and my unhappy father.

My mother quickly stripped us down, fussing at us the whole time. She told me 'Daddy would deal with me later' which meant I was probably going to get a whipping. She gave us a quick 'bird bath,' as she called it, out of the bathroom sink with soap and water, kind of like we had just done to Puddin and Moonpie in the woods.

"Now girls, go to the back bedroom. I have laid out matching dresses for you to put on." She cupped my chin in her hands, "Lee, I am counting on you to help Pam get dressed. Be big girls and don't embarrass me anymore."

"But Mama," I whimpered, "You know I can't tie me shoes by myself!"

"That's all right. I left your patent leather shoes out for you, and you can just slip those on. Just make sure Miss Pamsy Pansy has hers on the right feet. She kissed Pam on top of the head and pushed us naked down the hallway wrapped in towels.

Dresses just alike! My mother was always doing that to us, and I hated it. It wouldn't be so bad, but she liked the colors I did not like. Sure enough, when we got to the bedroom, two little ugly dresses were spread out on the bed for us with underwear and socks. The dresses were mint green with pink plaid stripes—who mixes those two colors? I thought it was horrid, but I did what my mother asked and dressed us like she wanted. I thought I was old enough to pick out what I wanted to wear, but honestly, I didn't like much of anything she ever bought me or had made for us. Of course, Pam put her shoes on the wrong foot and refused to let me help her. When we got to the dining room table, my mother put Pam on her lap and looked at me and said, "Oh Lee, you put her shoes on the wrong foot!"

"No, I didn't," I said, "She wouldn't let me help--she did it herself."

"She did it!" Pam pouted, pointing at me.

"No, I did not!" I said loudly.

"Lee, don't talk back to your mother," my father said nodding toward the preachers.

"But…"

"Pam, go have a seat and we will talk about all of this later," my mother said sternly.

We proceeded to have that meal that was I thought manna from heaven, and during the course of it, I heard things I have never forgotten, although the details are sketchy in my memory. I heard the preacher's wives comparing my mother's flair for fashion to Jackie Kennedy, our first lady. Mom had worn a pill box hat and square cut jacket in pastel colors like Mrs. Kennedy's the previous Sunday. All the ladies in the '60s wore lots of color, mostly pastels. However, the men in both the '50s and '60s wore only dark suits, white shirts, with narrow ties… narrow like their narrow minds. But times were about to change! The men were talking about President John F. Kennedy and about this black minister, Rev. Martin Luther King, Jr. I heard the respect and admiration for these men even though they disagreed with some of their politics. (You don't hear that today!) I also heard about how my grandfather had donated land for a black church to be built. When a black Baptist minister asked my grandfather if he would let him build a baptismal pool near a natural artesian spring on our farm to baptize his congregation, my dad said my grandfather was a little hesitant. Then the minister said, "What if I make it big enough for your kids and grandkids to use during the weekdays when we aren't using it?"

We grew up swimming in that pool with the coldest artesian spring water. At the time it seemed so big and now it looks so tiny! The pool was surrounded by cow pastures and not more than five hundred yards from the dairy barn. Not only did you have to get used to the cold water when you got in, you had to get used to the pungent smell of cow manure, too! We had many a birthday party, picnic and watermelon seed-spitting contest there, despite the smell. This conversation at the dinner table was the first time I had heard that it was built for blacks to be baptized. If that were the case and widely known, most white people have wouldn't have let their kids swim in it.

"What's baptized mean?" Pam spoke up.

"Rev. Jacobs, you want to explain that one?" my dad chuckled.

Rev. Jacobs dabbed his mouth with napkin. "Perhaps Joannie should. She is the only Baptist at the table!" He laughed and continued, looking directly at Pam, "Sweet child, you as a member of a Methodist family have already been sprinkled with Holy water. For Baptist, like how your mother was brought up, baptism is when you have asked Jesus to come into your heart and you have accepted Him as Lord and Savior. You go before the church to make that declaration before them and God, and you are dunked under water, and when you come up again, it signifies you are reborn as a Christian.

Immediately Pam's eyes lit up. "I want to do that! I want to be baptized and be dunked under the water! I just got some goggles and a mask this summer! Can we do that tomorrow!

Everyone at the table laughed. But that four-year old grew up to be extremely interested and sincere about her spirituality and religion. I am pretty certain she has been baptized by now, just in case sprinkling wasn't enough.

Not only was Mama's main course outstanding, so was the dessert. She served homegrown strawberries over her sour cream pound cake topped with homemade whipped cream. As we finished our dessert, my father told the preachers proudly, "You know, Joannie is the children's choir director at church. She just loves children. She has decided to start a kindergarten in our home this fall for five-year olds."

I almost choked on a strawberry. That was the first I had heard of it. I was supposed to start first grade which meant I would be riding a bus to school early in the morning and getting back late in the day. If she was having children over, I wanted to be in on it. I did not think it was one bit fair that my brother Trey and Pam would get to stay home and do fun things with Mama with a house full of children, and I had to go off with people I did not know. On the other hand, all I had seen my mother do was mope around for almost a year. I wasn't at all sure she was up to being a teacher.

My mind was a million miles away pondering all this as my mother was excitedly answering questions and being congratulated by the two pastors. Then my mother said, "Ok, I am going to let the children entertain you, so let's all go to the living room."

She always insisted we perform for guests until we were old enough to protest. Even my grumpy brother Trey would go along with it, but he said he would only do two songs. We stood on the hearth of our brick fireplace and waited for her cue. I don't know why she bothered to move her hands at us like she was leading an orchestra because none of us had a clue what it meant except when to start and stop. She first had us sing, "Jesus Loves the Little Children," and I made a mental note to see if Shine knew that song, too. Then Trey, who would become a veterinarian four decades later, said, "Mama, can we sing the one where I go 'ruff, ruff'?"

So, we had to do "How much is that Doggy in the Window." I think within a year we had performed that one at the county fair and the Farm Bureau Talent Show, and a couple of other places, all dressed alike, of course. As my mother directed us and sent Trey the cue for his part, I kept giggling thinking about how I had tried to direct it at the playhouse and "Ruff, ruff" was being said all over the place.

"How Much is That Doggie in the Window" went off without a hitch, and Trey did his part with great gusto. Afterwards, the preachers clapped, and we bowed because that was what we were used to doing.

Then my mother said, "Pam, why don't you do "Jesus Loves Me" by yourself. Lee is getting too giggly, and Trey did his two. Then we will be done."

Trey and I sat down on a chair together and left Pam on the hearth by herself. She put one hand on her hip and started bobbing her head and tapping her foot to get a beat going. My mother's hand was hanging in mid-air, ready to conduct her.

Pam closed her eyes, swung her head hung back and forth to her imaginary beat, and had her hand and head tilted like she was about to do "I'm a Little Tea Pot," not Jesus Loves Me". My mother looked confused. Then horrified as Pam belted out,

"There's just one Schlitz, yeah, yeah,
Nothing else comes near...

I honestly don't remember how far Pam got with it, but I do remember my mother sat there with her mouth wide open, hand still in mid-air, unable to speak. The preachers could not help themselves. They were slapping their knees, laughing, accusing my mother of setting it up on purpose, expressly for their entertainment. My father was totally embarrassed and started blaming me for putting Pam up to singing the beer commercial, so I grabbed Trey's hand and scrambled out of the room.

Trey and I sat in his room laughing about it until the company left. I told Trey about how Pam had sung the beer commercial earlier in the day for my little black friends and had pronounced "Schlitz" like "shits." Part of me was so proud of her for finally pronouncing it right and not saying "shits" in front of Rev. Jacobs and the other preacher. The other part of me could not imagine what possessed her to sing that instead of 'Jesus Loves Me'! The only thing I could figure is that the little brat enjoyed the laughter and the attention we had given her earlier in the day, and she sought the same reaction from an adult audience. She loved being the center of attention! She also loved blaming me for things she did, whether it was punishable or not, and more times than not, got away with it!

Sure enough, as soon as our company left, my daddy came in the bedroom and took off his belt, and I got a whipping I never forgot. I got about four licks for every charge. The litany of charges he bellowed out included: not coming home when called, talking back to my mother, using the 'n-word', especially in front the preachers, and, last but not least, putting Pam up to singing the Schlitz commercial. Of course, I did not do the latter, but as usual, Pam sure told them I did.

CHAPTER FOUR

~Adeline~fall of 1962

"You never know how strong you are until being strong is the only choice you have."

Bob Marley

In the last half of 1962, Marilyn Monroe, Eleanor Roosevelt, and my mother Ruth Jackson Reddick died. The only one mattered to me or my daddy or my six brothers and sisters was my mama. Her gorgeous black hair was wavy and smooth from the paper bag rollers she made and rolled in her hair each night. Her beautiful chestnut skin was always warm against my cheeks when she hugged me; and her twinkling eyes always seemed to be smiling, even when she was in pain or sad. For me, at 'leven years old, she was both my rock and life raft edging me toward a dream of some unknown shore in the distant future. For my daddy, it was a living nightmare to have his loving wife snuffed out at only 43 years old. After Mama died that November, Daddy won't never the same.

Daddy gave me my name at birth, but my mama gave me my name I go by. Ever night my mama would do a devotion with us, help us say our prayers, and sing me to sleep, singing, "You are my sunshine, my only sunshine. You make me happy when skies are gray. You'll never know, dear, how much I love you. Please don't take my Sunshine away." I was her baby, her Sunshine Baby, or just plain Shine to ever one else.

Mama was an angel on earth to all our neighbors, not just to us. She was a lady of many talents: healing, sewing, cooking and more. Mothers would bring their sick babies to her. If a baby had thrush, she could quote scripture, blow in his mouth and the thrush would go away. If someone, white or black, had a baby or got sick or died, she didn't just cook one dish. No! She would cook a whole meal, put it all in a dishpan atop of her head, and walk it to their house. She was the best cook in Lee County. When she died, my daddy went into a deep depression. And he should have—he was too cheap to take mama to the doctor for her high pressure and her pressure got so high, she died complaining of hellacious headaches that no Goody Powder would touch and had a brain hemorrhage. Daddy was never the same after that. Peggy and I was the only chillun' left at home; she was just fifteen and I won't even twelve yet. Daddy quit doing anything 'round the house; so, Peggy and I had to cook, chop wood for the stove, clean house, tend the garden, milk the cow, slop the pigs, and tend the chickens, not to mention work in the daggum fields. There won't much time for school less it was raining. Any playing I do'ed, I had to sneak off to the woods to do it and won't much time for that either.

All my older brothers and sisters moved up North cause there ain't no future here working in the fields for no money. That year Daddy told me and Peggy that the US Supreme Court passed a law that say black people can ride on buses or trains or any kind of public transport and if we was a little older, he would jes put us on a bus. That planted a seed in my head, so I started planning my future to leave when I was older right then.

We'd done had such a good summer 'fore Mamma died, playing in the woods with the McDonald girls. I'd tried so hard to get Mama and Daddy to let me ask Miss Joannie about babysitting, but Daddy say I won't nothing but a baby myself, and Mama says they can't do without me in the fields or in the garden. Mama seem like she won't ever feeling good with headaches and her pressure so high. Peggy and I tried to do as much as we could. When we got up in the morning, we had to milk the cow and see about the chickens, gather the eggs, slop the pigs, and sweep the kitchen and the front yard. We doesn't have grass in the yard like white people. We just sweeps the dirt to keep down the weeds. We don't got no money to fertilize no grass and no money to paint no house neither so when you go by a sharecropper or tenant house, you knowed which ones those was!

After doing all that, if it gonna be raining, you can go on to school—walk to school. If it ain't raining, you had to go help Mr. Alvie in the field. My daddy, Colin, was one of Mr. Alvie's best friends and his head sharecropper. Sharecropping is when a farmer who owns the land and equipment has some poor sucker like my daddy go in with him to buy the seeds, fertilizer, ever thing you need to grow the crop. The sharecropper and his whole family works in the field making the crop until it be harvested. Then at the end of the year, usually near Christmas, they split what they make on the crop minus what it cost to make it. Only problem with that is the famer also deducted ever thing else the sharecropper borrowed from him during the year: doctor bill money, medicine money, money from the bill run up at the Rollins country sto', money to buy an old car, money, money, money. By the time it be settled, and the sharecropper family got his share, it ain't near enough to last you through the next month, never mind the next year!

Mr. Alvie always let my daddy do the figures in the ledger behind him. Ne'er one of 'em had a good education because both of them had to work all their entire lives. Mr. Alvie only went to fourth or sixth grade—I forget which. My daddy only went to 3rd grade, but he was pure genius, 'specially at math. And he could grow anything and build anything. My daddy grew sugarcane and made molasses;

Mr. Alvie kept bees and made honey and they traded. What one didn't grow in they garden, the other did, so they traded. Mr. Alvie helped daddy build us a smokehouse the year mama died. 'Fore then, we smoked our meats at Mr. Alvies' and make our chitlins when he make his. He and Mrs. Eltie was right good to us. But we still won't getting nowhere fast like things was. And when my Mama died, I was right sho' my whole world had stopped. Things just went from bad to worser. I cried and cried, and then I cried some more. Somebody done took my soul out and stomped on it and stomped on it, and I won't sure anyone ain't ever gonna be able to put it back in my body. I was all alone in my grief. My daddy jes worked his self to death in his sorrow and withdrew from me and Peggy, she jes got meaner and meaner. Ever body handle grief in a different way, I reckon; but look like somebody could have comforted a child. I turnt twelve shortly after Mama died, and I growed up fast.

Now don't get me wrong, we always had plenty of good food because we was hard workers. Daddy made sure of that. We always had our own garden, chickens, and hogs. And Lord, my Mama could make a good breakfast out of that: eggs, hot biscuits and ham with red-eye gravy, stone-ground grits from the corn, and flapjacks with Daddy's molasses. When Mama died, I missed her good breakfasts almost as much as the sound of her constant hymn singing and her tight hugs. We dressed our own chicken and pork for eating and went fishing in the river for fish and cleaned that ourselves, too. When Mama died, Peggy and I helped Daddy the best we could, but it won't the same. Daddy said he'd made sure he got home at a decent hour to protect us from boys and boogers. He said don't let no boys come 'round when he won't there and for Lawd sakes, don't ever let 'em kiss us cause he ain't raising no mo' chilren.

So, I said to Lee, "You know how womens get pregnant? It is from kissing!"

We had a pact: we were not going to kiss no boys!

One time, Daddy askt Mr. Alvie if he could borrow his horse, Old Dan, to plow our garden. Old Dan had a sway back and the biggest feet of any horse I ever seen. But having big feet sho' didn't make him the fastest! No sir! He was the slowest! Calm and slow.

Ain't nobody could plow a field straighter than my daddy and Old Dan. Mr. Alvie always let Daddy lay out his cotton and tobacco fields to be planted because he could get those rows so straight. "Per-cision," Mr. Alvie called it. My daddy had a knack for it and was the best at it.

Anyways, Daddy and Old Dan took all afternoon to plow the garden. Old Dan was so slow. We'd already worked all morning for Mr. Alvie before he done got the old horse, so when Daddy finished, he was plum wore out. So I noticed how tired he was and begged him, "Daddy, can I please ride the horse back to Mr. Alvie's. Can I please, please?"

"No, Shine. That's over two miles! You're too little to be doing that. I'll take him back"

"No, Daddy. I can take him. You need to rest. I know the way."

"No, Shine."

"Please, please, please, daddy! I'm twelve years old; old enough to do ever thing else 'round here. Please let me take him home."

"Well, ok, Shine. Tell Mr. Alvie I am wore out, and I sho' do appreciate it."

Even though it was late in the evening, it was hot enough to roast lizards. Daddy let Old Dan have a drink of water before we go and say he was probably hungry, too, so maybe he'd hurry up and get back to the barn. Ha! Ain't nothing gonna make that horse go any faster. That horse gonna go slow no matter if you got a cow prod after him.

Daddy helped me mount and gave me a straw hat and off the road we went. Now mind you, at my young age, two miles seemed like a hop and a skip since I was used to walking twice that to school; but to Old Dan two miles after plowing all day, he was not going to be hopping and skipping to get us anywhere. He was his usual old slow self, over the bend, over the creek and to the bridge, and round the turn to the big house, slower than molasses out of a mason jar. At twelve years old, I was so proud my daddy entrusted me to take Old Dan back all by myself. The truth is, Old Dan knowed the way.

The hot sun was twinkling through the pine trees as it set and before long my clothes were soaked from its heat. I was getting sleepy. All I could hear was, clip, clop, clip, clop, clip, clop. Occasionally, he would fart as he walked thub, thub, thub, thub, but even that was like a lullaby. Pretty soon, I done laid my head down on Old Dan's neck. His shoulders rocked me back and forth until 'fore I knowed it, I was sound asleep. Next thing I know, I heared a voice, "Shine! Shine! Wake up"

I peeked out of one eye. It was Mr. Alvie!

"You and Old Dan come all this way by yourself?" he chuckled at me.

I sho' was embarrassed, but he thought it right funny. Mrs. Eltie came out and askt me if I wanted some iced tea. I loved her sweet tea—reminded me of Mama's. She took me home in her nice new shiny, black car, and we laughed about how Old Dan found his way home by his self. She told me how much she missed my mama, but it won't near as much as I be missing her. When I got home, I wondered if Mr. Alvie would charge Daddy's sharecropping account for the use of Old Dan. If so, I sho' hoped it won't by the hour as slow as that creature be. Sound like you can't never get ahead sharecropping because you gonna always owe the man at the big house something. We sho' was grateful. What choice did we have? With no education, we was stuck. It was one step above slavery. They still owned us. Um huh. They still owned us.

CHAPTER FIVE

~Lee~6yrs./first grade/fall of 1962

*"Often when you think you're at the end of something,
you're at the beginning of something else."*

Fred Rogers

As the days started getting cooler and the leaves started turning red, yellow, and deep amber, my little black friends came to the woods less and less. I didn't mind much because my father had put a new play set with swings and a huge tractor tire filled with sand in our back yard. Looking back, I am sure this was in preparation for my mother's new kindergarten class, but Al, Pam, and I loved it and benefitted, too. Occasionally I would see my friends as we passed by the cotton fields. The cotton was in full bloom and ready to harvest. I begged my mother to let me pick cotton too, so that I could see them, but it would be several years before I was allowed. It would be a long time before I realized my friends did not beg their mothers to let them pick cotton—they had no choice!

Two weeks before I started first grade, my mother decided I needed to learn to tie my shoes. Unfortunately for me, Velcro was not used on shoes until the late 1960's and would not be popular until the 80's. Every day for two weeks, my mother would sit me on the bed and squat in front of me and say, "Now make one bunny ear, then another bunny ear, then tie them together. Now you try it."

My four-year old sister and five-year old brother sat on the floor and looked on as Mama tried to teach me. By the end of the first week, my brother was a pro, and my sister was doing fairly well for a four-year old. I, on the other hand, was only getting increasingly frustrated at not being able to tie my shoes; by the end of the second week, so was my mother! School was the next day!

"Laverne, come see if you can teach this child to tie her shoes. I give up. I don't understand why she's not getting it. I have to put the children to bed, and she has school tomorrow, for goodness sake!"

Daddy came in and put me on his lap. He was usually gruff but for some reason, he was really gentle with me that night.

"What seems to be the matter, young lady. You are so smart. Why can't you tie your shoes? I know you can do it."

"I can't see the bunny ears. Mama keeps talking about my bunny ears, but I don't see any!" I said, tearfully.

Dad chuckled a little, and said, "Do you know what a loop is?"

"Yes sir."

He wrapped his arms around me and picked up one of my shoes and one of my feet and placed the shoe on my foot. "OK, hold this loop, now make another loop, then wrap that one around this one and pull tight. There! You just tied your shoe! Now, let's do the next one!"

I was smiling from ear to ear. My father was, too. This was my first conscious memory that I think more like my father than my mother. I didn't know the half of it.

The next morning Mama stood by the road with me in the chilly fog at 5:30 am waiting for the school bus. I was wearing a horrid dark blue, hunter green, and red plaid dress. I hated green, but that was my mother's favorite color. I was thankful for the darkness, hoping no one would see me with my chopped off hair, snaggled front teeth in this ugly dress—or my mom—she still had on her green housecoat and had curlers in her hair!

My mother nudged me with her flashlight, "Here, you want to play with this until the bus gets here?"

I exchanged my pencils and notebook for the flashlight and shined the light all around. I saw a hoot owl up in the pine trees, a red fox in the woods, and a racoon scurrying across the road. Then I turned the flashlight on me. My knobby knees had bruises from playing, my skinny legs had welts from my last whipping, and I was still bronzed from the summer sun. And my shoes! After all that hullabaloo about me learning to tie my shoes, my mother made me wear my Sunday patent leather shoes to school!

"Are you excited about riding the school bus?" my mother asked.

"Yes, ma'am, I guess" I answered through chattering teeth.

"Oh, don't be scared. Your bus driver is David Lucas. You know him. He goes to our church. He will take good care of you."

"Does it have a heater, Mama? I am cold,"

"You are so cold-natured. I think drivers have a heater near them, so I will ask David if you can sit near the front."

About that time, we could hear the diesel bus squealing to a stop down the road and see the flashing lights in the dark through the fog.

"Ok, he's going to stop here next. You are going to love school!"

I wrapped my arms tightly around my mother's legs. "Hug me, Mama, hug me, bye-bye!"

She bent down and kissed me on cheek, "I love you. You are going to have a great day!"

The school bus pulled up and David opened the door and Mama flashed the light for me to climb up the steps.

"Well, hi there, little lady! Hi, Miss Joannie! I will take real good care of her," the driver said.

While they discussed the heater situation and my cold-bloodedness, I just stood there. Two older boys started taunting me about my shoes.

"You're mighty dressed up to be going to school," one said, as they both laughed.

The other one pointed to my shoes, "You sure you're not going to church, little lady?

"No, today is my first day of school," I said proudly.

"Well, well, well. You don't need those shiny shoes at school. Everybody will think you think you are better than them," the first one said, sticking his tongue out at me.

David closed to door of the bus and said, "Miss Lee, come sit over here on the heater beside me and wave bye-bye to your mama."

He started singing and driving, and I started bawling.

"My goodness! I'll quit singing if you will quit crying. Am I that bad?" David asked.

I giggled and smiled through my tears, "Those boys were making fun of my shoes."

He was at a stop sign, so he lifted my leg and looked at my shoe.

I gave him my saddest look and said pathetically, "the ones that you tie with bunny rabbit ears...well, my mama wouldn't let me wear those today."

"I think these shoes are the finest shoes this side of the Mississippi! Boy, these shoes sure are special and so is the girl in them," David said as he looked at my shoes and winked. Then he looked in his rear-view mirror at the bad boys and said, "Stop making her cry about her shoes. Those are mighty fine shoes!"

I had no idea where Mississippi was; but one thing I did know is that David Lucas would protect me on that school bus, and he could definitely sing!

"Can you please sing some more!" I said, wiping the tears away.

He sang, "Blue Suede Shoes".

And he let me sit on the heater and sang to us every day he was my school bus driver.

Our next stop was at our family's farm to pick up my aunt, Barbara Jane. She was my father's sister and just two years older than I. I was calmer once she joined us. Our bus had to pick up all the kids in the St Matthews and Turkey Creek communities for several schools in town. We finally reached Bishopville Primary school around 7:45 am. My aunt got off the bus with me and showed me to my room. Mrs. Eckley, my first-grade teacher, was waiting for me and Barbara Jane went on to her third-grade room. I sat down where I was instructed and started looking around. Many of the kids were talking to each other and obviously were friends. My eyes scanned the room. I didn't see any of my friends. The two white girls my age from church were not in my class. Where was Moonpie? None of my black friends from the farm were there. Come to think of it, Shine and Puddin weren't on the bus! I scanned the room again. No, I saw absolutely no one I knew. I started crying.

The boy behind me pulled the sash on my dress, completely untying the bow, as he said, "Hey, ugly, I don't remember seeing you in kindergarten. Where are you from?"

He didn't realize I was crying until I turned around. It never occurred to me that other children got to go to kindergarten. I thought that was something new my mother had started just that year.

"Where did you go to kindergarten," I said, thinking it was not at our house last year.

"At Mrs. Beard's house uptown."

"Oh. I live out in the country," I sniveled.

He laughed.

I made my way up to the teacher's desk and asked her through tears to please tie my sash.

She bent down and tied it and said sweetly, "Go have a seat so we can get started. I'm just about to read everyone a book. Would you like that?"

"No, Ma'am! I want you to call my mama to come pick me up," I wailed. "I am not ready for first grade. I forgot to go to kinner garden, so I don't know how to do *anything!*"

"Darling, you are very smart, that is why you are in my class. You know your colors, and your numbers and you can even write your name."

That didn't impress me. My four-year old sister could do most of that!

"Well, I don't know any of these kids and they all know each other. None of my friends are here. Where are Jackie and Debbie? And where are all the black kids?" I asked. I really had no intention of going if my friends were not there.

Mrs. Eckley cleared her throat, "Sweetie, the black children have their own schools. They can't come to ours. Maybe you will see your little white friends at recess."

I wasn't sure what recess was, but I still wanted to go home. I was crying so hard I could barely talk. "Please, please call my mama. I need to change my shoes."

The teacher looked down at me feet.

"Oh, those are pretty shoes."

"I want my Maaaaamaaaa!" I wailed.

The class laughed and that only made me cry more. I simply would not quit crying, so finally my teacher took me to the third-grade room with my aunt. Barbara Jane scooted over in her desk and made room for me. For a couple of hours, I sat with her until she convinced me to calm down and go back to my class. For almost six weeks, I started out almost every day crying and at some point, being sent to my aunt's room. I mostly cried about the unfairness of it all: that everyone else had friends there and I did not, that Trey and Pam got to stay with Mama, and I did not, that black people were not allowed to go to our school. I missed the farm. I missed my brother and sister. I missed my mama. But most of all, I missed my black friends in the woods. For a six-year-old, the grief was as real as losing my precious baby brother.

One day I got up to go to school and my mother was not there. She was at the hospital with my daddy and Trey. Lizzie was there and my grandmother, Miss Eltie, that I called Mama Mac.

"Your daddy took Trey with him to Sumter last night to pick up a deer head they'd had mounted trophy as a for Daddy Mac. A fellow didn't have any lights on his trailer or taillights on his tractor and your daddy came 'round a curve in the dark and ran right into him. Tore up the front of his car, broke his arm and his leg, threw little Trey in the foot of the car and his face is all cut up. The inside of his mouth is a mess," Mama Mac said.

"Are they alive?" I wanted to know.

"Yes, shug, they're alive. By the grace of God, they are both alive. I am not so sure about the other driver."

Back then, no law prevented children from sitting in the front seat with no seat belts. Trey's mouth was cut from the metal door of the heater located in the foot of the passenger side of the car. He had to have his mouth wired shut to reset his jaw. The impact was so hard it permanently offset the center line of his front teeth.

"Miss Eltie, I can stay with Lee if you thinking she shouldn't go to school today." Lizzie said.

"I want to see my brother. Can I go see him? Can I go see Daddy, too?" I begged. I wanted to see with my own eyes that my family was still alive, but Mama Mac left me with Lizzie. Lizzie rocked me like I was a baby until I quit crying.

She knew the way to my heart was food, so she said, "Why don't I make you some blueberry pancakes, and then we will get Miss Pam up to eat them with you, OK?"

"Lizzie, look...that's the lady that was our maid before you on that syrup."

"Betty McRay?" Lizzie chuckled. "That ain't Betty! That's Aunt Jemima!"

"She looks like her to me."

Pam and I barely finished gobbling down the pancakes with our Aunt Betty's syrup (as it came to be known), when Mama came in the door carrying Trey and Daddy hobbling in on crutches behind her. He had a cast on his leg and arm. Trey's face was swollen and bruised. He still looked dazed and was probably sedated somewhat. Pam took one look at Trey and said, "Is he going to die?"

CHAPTER SIX

~Adeline~1963

"The need for change bulldozed a road down the center of my mind."

Maya Angelou

I loved to go to school and to church, but the year after my mama died, I gots to go less and less. That was where you got to be with all your friends, at least the black 'uns, and learnt all about what was going on out there in the world. Peggy and I had to walk to school and take our own lunch. We even went in the snow! But that won't as bad as when a white school bus went by and went through mudpuddles, splashing us with muddy water on purpose. Half the time, we was already too far to go back home and change clothes.

Our school was a one-room schoolhouse where all the grades was. At our school, the big boys and girls would help the teacher with the little boys and girls. I liked it when I got to help Mrs. Alphonso or Mrs. Gregg teach. Ours was the first schoolhouse in Lee County in that neck of the woods for black chilrun long before us came to it. Later it became the home of the McDonald's maid, Miss Lizzie, and then we started going uptown to school. I often wondered if Mary McLeod Bethune had anything to do with our little old schoolhouse because the white people sure didn't seem to have any interest in us getting educated. Miss Mary was one of the first famous black women I ever knowed anything about, and she was from right near here in Mayesville, SC, over near Sumter. She started lots of schools for black chilrun over there and became the first black woman, maybe even first of any women, to be the head of a college. She be the head of Bethune-Cookman College in Florida. She believed in an education just like my beloved mama did. I was determined I was going to get mine, somewhere, somehow.

After school, after church, and even after working in the fields some days, we'd get up enough black kids to have a baseball game. It was one of my favorite past times and I was pretty good at it. We had plenty of fields around us to make a baseball diamond; and Mr. Alvie let us make one, the church had one and we had one at school.

One day I was playing ball near Mr. Alvie and Miss Eltie's strawberry patch, and they sent Lee over to see if I wanted to help them pick berries. I was in the middle of a fight with a boy about twice my size who been stealing bases unfairly all day, and I'd had enough.

"When I done tagged second base, and nobody ain't moving off third, you is supposed to stay there. There ain't no stealing away if the base ain't empty. You be done it three times and we done told you not to. What's wrong with you? You can't run all over the farm to avoid me getting you out!"

"Well, you ain't caught me yet!"

"If you can't play by the rules, you can take your black hinney home, you hear me?"

"Well, little girls don't have no business out here playing baseball, maybe you should take yours home, sassafras!"

Lee interrupted us, "Adeline, come here a second."

She whispered in my ear, "I found out its not kissing that gets a girl pregnant; it's arguing. Quit arguing with him! Oh my gosh! If you argue with boys, you will wind up pregnant!"

I pulled away from her and looked at Lee to see if she was being comical on purpose. She be concerned and dead serious.

"Who done told you that?"

"I dunno. I just observed it. My daddy, I guess."

"Dear heart, Vern know better than that. That's not how you get pregnant!" I said as I laughed so hard, tears came out of my eyes.

"Well, then how, smarty pants?"

"From kissing, ever body knows that. I done told you that."

"Nuh uh! I have seen it several times on the farm. Just this morning, Daddy put a bull in the pen with some heifers and I asked him why that bull was jumping up all over the lady cows. He said they were heated, and the bull was just arguing with them. When I asked why the bull was arguing with them, he said to try to get them pregnant. And a couple of weeks ago I saw Daddy Mac's sow arguing with the pigs, too, and now they're pregnant. You ever seen them kissing?"

I pondered that a second. "You really think that is how? I still think kissing's got something to do with it."

I heard snickering behind us. We thought we was whispering, but ever body seemed to be listening in on us.

"I don't know," she said, "I told you that my daddy argues with Mama a lot and he's already gotten her pregnant four times. You better be careful."

She was as dog gone serious as she could be. When she left, the whole ballfield was in stitches. Then that fool I was arguing with tried to kiss me! I couldn't get to the strawberry patch fast enough to tell Lee what happened. And, of course, we áte more strawberries than we picked.

Shortly after that, Mr. Rollins that ran the country store told me I could get any candy I wanted on a certain shelf in his store. Daddy wouldn't let me spend any money, but Mr. Rollins always be nice to me. So, I decided I wanted a pack of baseball cards. Daddy said to put them back, he won't paying for them; but Mr. Rollins already said I could have them. I couldn't open them fast enough. Daddy walked on out to talk to the mens at the front like he usually do, so I stayed inside, opening my candy. Popped that bubble gum right in my mouth and I was looking at the cards that came in them. I seen Mr. Rollins looking over my shoulder and I turned the top card so he could see it.

"Woowee, gal! You hit the jackpot on your first deck! This the first pack you got?"

"Yes, sir."

"You know who that is?" He said pointing to the black ball player in the card.

"No sir, who?"

"That is Jackie Robinson. Not only is he the first Black professional ball player in the Big Leagues, but he also just got named to the National Baseball Hall of Fame! He is breaking all kinds of barriers for Black people! You need to hang on to that card. It will be worth a lot of money some day! Probably is now!"

I went running out of the store, looking for my daddy.

"Daddy, Daddy, look what I got!"

He took one look at it and tried to grab it out of my hand.

"That ain't for little girls. Give that here!" My daddy yelled at me.

Mr. Rollins shot out of that store and grabbed the card back from Daddy and handed it back to me."

"That gal didn't get the penny canny like you told her to."

"Now, Colin, that card is most certainly Shine's. You wouldn't even buy it for her. That was my gift to her. From all accounts, your gal is a really good ballplayer. I don't know when her birthday is, but let's just say it's her birthday gift. You probably don't even know when that is.

And that was that. But I 'spect Daddy took it and sold it to somebody after several years because when I went to move, I couldn't find it. But I was always grateful for Jackie Robinson, and it made me love baseball even more.

At church, we not only learned about the Bible and how to be good Christians, but we also learned what was going on in the world. Since not hardly a one of us had a TV, we learned what was going on in the Black community, in politics and anything else that mattered to Black people at church mostly. We had radios, but they was stations owned by white people so you onliest heard their perspective or maybe didn't hear it at all. One of the people I heard about at church was Rev. Martin Luther King, Jr. Our pastor kept us up on Rev. King's protests and speeches and told us about he stood for love and peace, not for hate and war. As my mama said, you can get a lot more sweetness out of an old billy goat with honey and sugar than you can with vinegar and salt and a cow prod. And you know what? One Sunday in April 1963 the preacher told us about the civil rights demonstrations in Birmingham, Alabama. I remember it because that is where my mama was born! The black peoples was having a peaceful demonstration and the police used dogs and cattle prods on them. Cow prods! Then, in May, it got worse! The pastor told us some school children were on their way to boycott a school that won't integrated, and the police unleashed dogs and high-powered water hoses on them. It goes without saying that lead to a race riot. I sho' wished my mama was still alive to have a word a prayer with them crazy white people. She could tell you to go to hell with honey and sugar and make you glad you took the trip without using nary a bad word!

One of the things Rev. King said that always stuck with me is, "Take the first step in faith. You don't have to see the whole staircase, just the first step." I kept that in mind when I started most scary things in my life. Our church sold pictures of Rev. King to raise money for the church and I bet every black home in Lee County had one! Daddy had Rev. King's quotes on little postcards he gave us, too.

That fall, my sister Peggy was at Mrs. Eltie's doing her ironing, and I came with Daddy to help Mr. Alvie at the smokehouse. We was making chitlins in a big old black kettle over a fire in the back yard. If you don't know what chitlins is, it's the guts of a hog; and when you clean them our real good, boil them, then deep fry 'em, I promise you, they sho' is good! Daddy let me deal with the chitlins and cracklings while he and Mr. Alvie got the bacon, fat back, pig's feet and all dressed down, and then I was going to help them smoke some hams. But all the sudden, Peggy and Mrs. Eltie came to the backdoor yelling for us to come watch the tv set. She ain't ever askt us to watch her tv with her before, so we didn't know what was happening. Mr. Alvie said World War Three must be done started. When we got to the television, which was still in black and white, Mrs. Eltie and Mr. Alvie sat down and we just stood there staring, amazed at what we saw. Mrs. Eltie said it was Rev. Martin Luther King, Jr. in Washington, DC, at the Lincoln Memorial, and that it was a speech that we was all going to remember, so be quiet and listen.

A humongous crowd of mostly black people was gathered as far as you could see! Rev. King was powerful and commanding as he did his "I Have a Dream" speech. I 'spose we came in about the middle of his speech. I memorized that speech and to this day I can recite most of it.

"And so even though we face the difficulties of today and tomorrow, I still have a dream. It is a dream deeply rooted in the American dream.

I have a dream that that one day that one day this nation will rise up and live out the true meaning of its creed: 'We hold these truths to be self-evident, that all men are created equal.'

I have a dream that one day on the red hills of Georgia the sons of former slave and the sons of former slave owners will be able to sit down together at the table of brotherhood.

I have a dream that one day even the state of Mississippi, a state sweltering with the heat of injustice, sweltering with the heat of oppression, will be transformed into an oasis of freedom and justice.

I have a dream that one day my four little children will live in a nation where they will not a be judged by the color of their skin but by the content of their character."

I have a *dream* today!" Reverend Martin Luther King bellowed as he lifted his heels up and shook his fists, and the crowd roared.

I glanced around the room and Mr. Alvie's eyes were moist and Daddy and Peggy had tears running down they cheeks! Mrs. Eltie was gritting her teeth and I couldn't tell what she was thinking. When Rev. King started talking about little black kids holding little white kids' hands, I wanted to tell Mrs. Eltie we was already holding hands with her grands, but I didn't know how she'd take that. But I knowed we had a long way to go. I wanted an education, Daddy wanted to vote and none of us wanted to feel like slaves. We wanted to indeed feel free, free at last. I couldn't see the top of the stairs, but I knew Rev. King had gotten us up the staircase quite a ways that day.

A few Sundays after that, I learnt at Sunday School the Ku Klux Klan had bombed the First Baptist Church in Birmingham and killed four little black girls as they got ready to do their lesson on "the love that forgives." Lord, help me but it were getting harder. Those girls could have been me if my grandma had not moved back to South Carolina when my mama was little. Their names were Denise McNair, Carole Robertson, Addie Collins, and Cynthia Wesley. Now I knowed their names 'cause I prayed for them for a long time. I prayed they'd be angels over all us little black girls left on this earth. I prayed no white people would hate us so bad they'd bomb our church like they did that 'un.

Not long after that, I was spending the night with my cousin, Sally. We was playing in her room, and her mother starting yelling for us to get under the bed, get under the bed! She said the Ku Klux Klan be outside the house! We didn't see them from under the bed, but she told us they was hooded and all in white and carrying torches. She didn't know what they was up to. She thought they gonna burn the house down. After what I heared at church, I was sure terrified for my life. Now I tell you, I ain't never been so scared! Later I found out the KKK had a meeting on Lee's daddy's land without his consent and burned a cross. About burned Vern's hay field up! Her daddy was sho' mad about that!

In October of 1963, Martin Luther King, Jr. was the youngest person to ever receive the Nobel Peace Prize. He won it for his efforts to try to solve racial prejudices with non-violent protests. Rev. King was going to be our savior, and I could see change a-coming! We was going to be free at last!

CHAPTER SEVEN

~Lee~7yrs old/fall of 1963

"Perhaps there is a limit to the grieving that the human heart can do. As when one adds salt to a tumbler of water, there comes a point where no more will be absorbed."

Sarah Waters, The Little Stranger

Just as I was getting used to attending school, we had a national emergency going on that caused security concerns for school children. President Kennedy decided that the of presence Soviet missiles in Cuba was not acceptable as Cuba is only 90 miles from Florida. The problem the USA had was how to remove them without initiating a bigger conflict and perhaps even a nuclear war. President Kennedy weighed his options and decided on a blockade and then delivered an ultimatum that the missiles be removed. He was prepared to use military force if necessary. People all over the world waited for Russia's response to his demands. Meanwhile, we were having "duck and cover" drills at school. The teacher would yell out, "Drop!" at random and the students had to dive underneath their desks in case of an airstrike. At other times, the fire alarm would go off and the teachers would herd us to the hallway to sit in the hall with our heads between our legs. What six- year-old would not have been rattled? Fortunately, the Soviet Union ships sent in response stopped short of the blockade, and both sides worked out an agreement to remove missiles as long as we did not invade Cuba.

I still wanted to go home to my mama, and my teacher was still sending me to my aunt's third grade class a few hours a day. I could even do a lot of their work, thanks to my aunt. I was bored to death in mine and still had not made many friends.

I lived for the holidays and breaks to spend more time in our playhouse with my friends and with my own toys. For the Christmas of 1962, I got an etch-a-sketch, lots of crayons and coloring books, my first Barbie and her friend Midge with a wardrobe for both, and a bicycle. Pam had also gotten some Barbies and a little red Radio wagon for Trey and me to pull her in, though most of the time Pam preferred to carry her toys in it. Trey got lots of airplanes and stuff about Cape Canaveral which launched a childhood interest in rockets. I could not wait to go to the playhouse to see what my friends had gotten for Christmas and show them some of what Pam and I got. I kept going each day during Christmas break until one day all of them showed up. I was pulling Pam in her little red wagon had a couple of Barbies and the etch-a-sketch and some coloring books with us,

"Hi, girls, we came to see what Santa Claus brought y'all!" I said excitedly.

Moonpie and Puddin hung their heads and just giggled. Shine said, "there ain't no Santa.

"Is so, "said Pam.

Shine started laughing, "Honey chile, don't you know Santa is your mommy and daddy?"

"Shine, let her believe in Santa as long as she can," I cautioned.

"I know there is too a Santa," Pam said, "Look at all these gifts we got!"

Moonpie said, "If there's a Santa, why ain't we got no gifts?"

"What do you mean?" I asked.

"We ain't got nothing for Christmas," Moonpie said again. "Is you deaf?"

"Maybe you was bad," Pam offered.

Moonpie just glared at her and Puddin said real low, but emphatically, under her breath, "She ain't been bad."

Shine, ignoring their mood, said real cheerfully, "Well, daddy always makes all our gifts. Wanna know what I got?"

"What did you get?" I asked, sorry I had asked them about Christmas at all.

"He made us a seesaw, a jump board, and a sling shot, and a telephone with some tin cans. You know, we could use one of those here!" Shine sounded excited as if she had gotten the most expensive toys in the store.

The see saw had been in their yard for almost a year, but I didn't say anything. It was an old barrel with a plank of wood over it and I had been begging daddy to make us one.

"How do you make a telephone? We ain't got one at home. Sho' would be nice to have one here." Puddin said.

"Find me two tin cans and I will show you!"
Shine then stabbed the end of the cans with the end of an old board with a nail sticking out to make a hole. Then she tied tobacco twine through the cans connecting the two cans. Shine was always carrying tobacco twine and she always seemed to be using it. The real reason she carried the twine was to play Jacob's Ladder when she got bored. I knew because she taught me one day.

"Here, go way over there and try out our new phone," Shine said to Puddin.

Puddin took the can and walked to the other end of our little playhouse.

"Can you hear me?"

"Loud and clear."

Of course, we all had to take turns trying it, and I remember being surprised at how that simple little homemade toy could amplify your voice. I was amazed at

Shine, and so proud that our playhouse had a telephone. I would bet not many of my friends had playhouses with telephones!

I winked at Shine. "You know, Puddin and Moonpie, I think Santa left your gifts at our house. These coloring books and crayons must be for y'all because we already have some," I said and gave the all the crayons and four coloring books from the wagon. Pam nodded in agreement, handing them to me.

"I will give you something for Knee-Boy later," I said. thinking I would give him some toys Trey had outgrown. "How is he doing?"

Moonpie immediately burst into tears. Puddin put her arm around her, tears streaming down her cheeks, too. She swallowed hard for a minute and gritted her teeth before she spoke.

"Knee-Boy's dead. He done died of polio 'bout two weeks ago.

We stood in stunned silence with the sound the soft whimpers of the girls and the rustling of the winter leaves for a minute while the news sunk in. Shine was still hurting over the loss of her mother, and I over the loss of my baby brother. We knew the pain. Oh, how we knew their pain! The girls dropped to the moss in each other's arms, and Shine and I did the same. Pam went around to all of us hugging each one of us, still too young to comprehend it all. Grief united us and our souls were raw and bare, and our skin color did not matter, not that it ever had to us. We all reached out and held hands while Shine led us in prayer. It was one of the saddest yet most profound moments of my life to this day.

When I went home, I had to get my mother to explain what polio was to me. She explained that crippled Mrs. Truett, the lady who bought us our Watkins flavorings that mom used in all her delicious pound cakes was on crutches from having polio as a child. She said it paralyzes muscles.

Polio paralyzed Mrs. Truett's legs and Knee-Boy's lungs. He could no longer breathe on his own. She also told me that up until then there had been no cure, but our family was scheduled to go get our first vaccination soon.

Sure enough, in early 1963 our family went to the cafeteria at the high school to eat little pink sugar cubes to keep from getting polio. Jonas Salk had previously invented a vaccine that was done with a shot containing a weakened virus, but it had some complications and was sometimes not effective. Albert Sabin had found a way to inoculate the public with an inactivated version of the virus that goes through the stomach first. This is the first time I remember being interested in microbiology, although I did not know the word for it. I was only seven years old. I was asking my parents questions about it incessantly because I was so fascinated that something you could not see with your eye could wreck that much havoc with your body or even kill you. However, they thought I was obsessed with fear of becoming sick and becoming a hypochondriac. I was also worried about all the Black people on the farm and kept asking Daddy if he would bring them to be vaccinated, or "take them some sugar cubes." He finally told me that he and Daddy Mac took care of it. Just to make sure, I stole some sugar cubes from the drug store soda fountain counter one after noon and took some to the girls in the woods. I figured since I got them at the drug store, they had the "cure" in them. I asked Mr. Kirkley if his sugar cubes could cure polio, and I am pretty sure he saw me grab a few as he made my treat.

"Princess, that ice cream float your mama just bought you will cure just about anything," he said with a wink.

And I do believe he was right. A fountain soda with a scoop of vanilla ice cream is way better than chicken noodle soup.

Shortly before my birthday that March, Mama took me to the health department to get some more vaccinations for school. We all got mumps, measles, and chicken pox back then before you could be vaccinated for them and we got a smallpox vaccination and tetanus shot before you started to school, so I am not sure which one I was getting. I was sitting on the examination table and a nurse came in, talking to me like I was a baby.

"OK, sweet girl, I am just going to roll up your little sleeves and you won't feel a thing. See the little bunny rabbit?"

Oh no. I don't see a bunny. I just see a cotton ball in her hand, fake-bouncing toward me

"No," I said,

"Yes, see the little bunny, bounce, bounce, bounce...he's lost his ears!"

I look down at my shoes. I see my shoelaces are tied.

"You mean the loops on my shoes?" I asked, quite confused. "*Ouch*!"

"There you go, now that didn't hurt a bit, did it?"

"Yes ma'am, it did! Why do you lie about everything?" I mumbled out loud.

To myself, I thought, "What *is* the thing with adults and bunnies?"

The next day was my birthday. I always knew when my birthday was coming because our yard told me: the daffodils were blooming and the buds on the dogwoods were starting to open. Guess what kind of cake my mom made me! A bunny rabbit cake! I thought she was making fun of me. What is it with adults and bunny rabbits? I kept looking at the cake to see if I was supposed to see a hidden meaning. Well, it did have bunny ears.

"Can we eat it?" I asked, confused.

I got promoted to second grade that fall and felt a bit more comfortable that Trey was on the bus and going to school, too. We had a routine of getting a snack when we came in from school and watching our little black and white tv in our parent's bedroom with Pam. Our favorite program was Spaceship CH, a children's show with Howdy Doody and the Little Rascals reruns with Spanky and Our Gang on it. Spanky and our Gang was a group of black and white friends with a club house. I would dream for hours of how Sunshine and I could have a clubhouse like theirs, not realizing that in a way, our outdoor playhouse was very much like theirs. I was very naïve about how rare friendships were like that in the South, and Spanky and our Gang only made ours seem even more normal.

One day Trey and I came home from school and found a note attached to the TV. It said, "Lee, I need you to be a big girl and look after Trey until Daddy or I come to pick you up. I had to take Pam to the hospital. She has pneumonia. Love, Mama"

I could read it, well, everything but "pneumonia". I started crying. First Little Roger, then Knee-Boy. My mind was spinning. I didn't know what pneumonia was, but it started with a "p" like polio; and the last time I had a sibling go to a hospital, they didn't come back! And neither did Shine's mother. Trey wanted to know why I was crying.

"I don't know, I think Pam is dying. Mama took her to the hospital. If she were just sick, I don't think she would just leave us here by ourselves."

Trey started wailing. He loved his little sister. I tried to console him, but he ran to his room and got in bed and sobbed. I sat there and had a word of prayer with God...I had had enough of this death stuff and told Him as much.

By the time I finished my prayer, which was rather long, my mother arrived. Trey and I ran to the door to see what happened and find out what the big word with a "p" meant. Mama explained that the doctors were treating Pam with antibiotics, and she would be alright. She was very congested and had a bacterial infection in her lungs. I asked if bacteria were so tiny you couldn't see them, just like the viruses in polio. She said yes, they were both called microbes. Neither of us knew I would grow up to be a microbiologist, but once again all the talk about these unseen organisms that could harm the body certainly planted the seed.

Pam had been out of the hospital only a couple of weeks, however, when another death did hit, and in a big way. In November of 1963, we had been at school for about half the day when suddenly, teachers were crying, and we were being sent home.

President Kennedy had been shot!

Trey and Pam and I piled on our parent's bed and watched the little black and white television broadcasting the assassination over and over. Handsome young President Kennedy and the stylish First Lady had been riding in an open-air limo through downtown Dallas toward the Dallas Trade Market where he was scheduled to give a speech. As the convertible traveled passed the Texas School Book Depository, the president was shot by someone we later found out to be Lee Harvey Oswald. The image of Mrs. Kennedy scrambling over the back of the convertible to gather the top of her beloved husband's head that had blown off has stayed with me for a long time. John F. Kennedy had been president for 2 years, 10 months and 2 days and had two kids around our age. He was just 46 years old. Our whole nation mourned, Republicans and Democrats alike. Through the whole weekend, grief blanketed the whole community with a thick mourning everywhere you went, whether it was the grocery, the library, or church. Nothing was on television but replays of the assassination, speeches by Kennedy, and then his funeral that Monday. So many memorable scenes aired, and I have never forgotten them since, and I was only seven years old. One thing is for sure: grief united us, just like it had us little girls in the playhouse.

CHAPTER EIGHT

~Adeline~1963

"Play is the work of children. It's very serious stuff! "

Bob Keeshan (Captain Kangaroo)

In November of 1963, I got me a ride up to the McDonald's house to see Mr. Vern, Lee's daddy. The one-year anniversary of my mama's death was the week before and my daddy was getting worser and worser. Grief, I guess, had done took his spirit and his will to work. I didn't want Mr. Alvie to see him like he was. Mr. Vern had to go on after losing one of his chilrun. I thought he might have some words that might do some good with my daddy. Daddy had just got plain mean. He acted like he was mad with the whole world.

When I knocked on the door, Miss Joannie came to the door and looked just awful with her pretty self. She'd been crying!

"Come in, Shine. Are you by yourself?"

"Yessum. I came to talk to Mr. Vern. I see his truck is here. But ain't nobody at the farm. Ever thing alright?" I asked, looking around.

"Oh sweetheart, he is in the family room, glued to the television...Have you not heard? Someone shot the president today!"

"Which president? Mr. Kennedy? Oooh! No wonder my daddy so upset! Oh Lawd! Is he dead?" I asked.

"I am afraid so. They are swearing in the vice-president as president now. Shine, if you aren't in a big hurry, I have a favor to ask you. Lizzie, our maid, is sick and I was going to let Lee walk down to her house with some soup and cornbread and her money for helping us this week. Do you mind walking down there with Lee?"

"Yes, ma'am. I sho will." I told Miss Joannie. I was a good bit older than Lee although we was about the same size. I'm sure she didn't want her walking down there by herself, but I was used to walking ever where round here at ten or so.

She called Lee to come go with me and offered me a piece of hot cornbread. It was all fluffed up, not flat like the hoe cakes my mama taught us to make. It sho was good, with butter all over it. I askt her if I could have another piece, it was so good.

"Now Miss Lizzie probably doesn't know about the president yet," Miss Joannie said. "Lee, do you think you and Shine could tell her? And tell her that if she is feeling better, she can come to work up here some Monday and watch his funeral on television with us. Most everything will probably be closed Monday. I had planned to take her to the doctor on Monday, but I am sure he will be closed, too. Maybe just tell her I will go by and check on her Monday and see if she needs to go to the hospital since the doctor's office won't be open; but if she is well, I can bring her back here instead."

"Mama, I can't remember all that!" Lee told her mama.

"I got it! I got it!" I said. "Take this here to Miss Lizzie, see if she still be sick. Tell her you gonna come check on her Monday, and either you gonna take her to the hospital or to work here, right?"

"And tell her that President Kennedy was assassinated," Miss Joannie said.

"How 'bout I jes say he got shot and he is dead, ok?"

Miss Joannie put ever thing in a basket for us to take to Miss Lizzie, and Lee and I walked about a mile to her house. When we got there, Lizzie had made designs in the dirt with the broom in the yard and had pots of flowers on the porch of her unpainted tenant house. It sho looked good. We knocked on the door and Miss Lizzie invited us in.

Lee ran to Lizzie and hugged her tight. "I miss you so much," Lee said.

"Aww, you ain't missed me…you missed my cooking," Lizzie chuckled.

"We brought you some of Mama's cooking. She can make a mean cup of vegetable soup and pretty good corn bread! And your money is in here, too. This is the first time I've been in your house," Lee said, looking around. "Is that a picture of your father?"

Lizzie and I both laughed as she pointed to the hero of our time.

"No, shug, that be Rev. Martin Luther King. If you don't know who he is, you sho' will know soon. Do you know who that one is?"

Lizzie pointed to JFK.

"Yep. That is John F. Kennedy, our president. Or was. He got shot today, Lizzie—assass'nated—and he is dead!" Lee said.

"Yes, baby, I done heared it on the radio. That's partly why I's sick," Lizzie exclaimed.

"Well, if you ain't sick on Monday, Miss Joannie wants you to work," I said.

"Chile, Mr. Kennedy still gonna be dead on Monday, so I reckon I still be sick on Monday, too."

"She say you can watch all of it on tv," I told her.

"I always watch my stories on the tv while I am ironing or cleaning the bedroom," Lizzie said as she took down the president's picture and dusted it.

"Lizzie, the president's funeral will be on tv on all three channels. I don't think your soap opera's gonna be on, "Lee informed her. "Sounds like you have a cold. You don't have to come if you don't feel like it."

Yeah, back then, we only had three tv stations! Can you believe that!

Lizzie said she would see how she felt, and we headed back to tell Miss Joannie. On the way, Lee asked me about them pictures.

"Shine, why do black people have pictures of Martin Luther King and John F. Kennedy on the wall, but don't have any pictures around of their family?"

"We don't have no camera and we ain't got no money for pictures," I laughed.

"White folks have pictures all over the place. Our whole kitchen wall and the hallway are both filled with family pictures. We get them made at school, at church, and then we have several cameras we use as well as an 8mm-movie camera," Lee told me. "We don't have pictures of that Black man or John F. Kennedy on the wall, though. I think that is weird!" Lee said, looking at me like something be wrong with me.

"You know what's weird?" I said, "that we works twice as hard as white folk, and they gets all the money. You know, I saw you and Barbara Jane sitting on the porch in the shade shelling peas with Miss Eltie a couple of weeks back while me and Peggy were breaking our backs out in the hot sun next to the big house picking cotton. I wished I could trade places with you."

Lee didn't say nothing. We walked on a ways and I said, "I don't have any family I *want* a picture of right now.... Daddy and Peggy have been down right mean to me ever since Mama died. My aunts and my grandma, where they be? Nobody been helping us out."

Lee reached over and grabbed my hand and made me stop. She hugged me.

"My daddy is mean to me, too," she said. "When I get grown and have children, I am going to be real sweet to mine. Children should love their mother and father."

"Yeah, that be one of the Ten Commandments, ain't it? Guess I am going to have to work on that one. But I sho' loved my mama," I said.

"When we were shelling peas, we were listening to y'all singing out in the fields. It was so beautiful. Teach me that song, Shine."

"Dear heart, which one would you like me to teach you? *Swing Low, Sweet Chariot* or *Stand by Me on this Lonesome Journey?*"

We sang '*Swing Low*,' swinging our arms to the rhythm. Ain't nobody listening to us but the birds chirping in the trees. Occasionally, you could hear them going, "Caw, Caw," like they liked what they heared.

I instructed Lee just to sing the same line every time I sang a line. So, I would sing one or two lines of *Swing Low, Sweet Chariot* and then she would sing the same line: "Coming for to carry me home." It go like this:

Swing low, sweet chariot,
Comin for to carry me home;
Swing low, sweet chariot,
Coming for to carry me home.

I looked over Jordan
And what did I see,
Coming for to carry me home,

A band of angels comin' after me,
Coming for to carry me home.

Swing low, sweet chariot,
Comin for to carry me home;
Swing low, sweet chariot,
Coming for to carry me home.

If you get there before I do,
Comin for to carry me home;
Tell all my friends I am coming too,
Coming for to carry me home.

Swing low, sweet chariot,
Comin for to carry me home;
Swing low, sweet chariot,
Coming for to carry me home.

Sometimes I'm up, sometimes I'm down,
Comin for to carry me home;
But still my soul feels heavenly bound,
Coming for to carry me home.
Swing low, sweet chariot,
Comin for to carry me home;
Swing low, sweet chariot,
Coming for to carry me home.

"Do you know *Jesus Loves the Little Children*? Let's sing that one."
Lee always wanted to sing that one.

We made plans to meet at the playhouse on Monday since there won't be no school nar work. By the time we was walking down the long driveway to the McDonalds' place, we was still holding hand's singing and giggling without a care in the world. We was singing 'Mares eat oats and does eat oats and little lambs eat ivy.' Whoever wrote that song was crazy.

Now I tell you who was really crazy! Them Beatles! Not long after President Kennedy died and Lyndon Johnson was made president, the Beatles came to the USA and them white girls went fool over them. They had long hair like poor white trash and gyrated their hips like Mr. Elvis. And the white girls fell out like they was at a church tent meeting. They start yelling and crying and swooning---you couldn't even hear the boys singing for the girls screaming. Us black girls liked them, too, but we liked dancing to Chubby Checker, Little Richard, and James Brown. We liked listening to Otis Redding, Jerry Butler, and The Temptations. And the white folk liked all them, too; they just won't ready for them to sit down and have a meal with them or put their hiney in the same bathroom.

But I am getting ahead of myself. When Monday rolled around, we did what we planned to do: have a dress up tea party, just me and Lee, in the playhouse. I brought some fried baloney sandwiches, and Lee brought some peanut butter and banana on mayonnaise sandwiches and a Pepsi-Cola for us to split. Since it was a tea party, I don't know why neither of us thought to bring any daggum iced tea, but Pepsi was a treat for us cuz neither of us gots to have sodas much! It was a cool fall day, so we both wore long pants and long-sleeved shirts and brought a sack of dress-up clothes. The stage was still set up, but we needed a little table near the couch. I found an old milk crate and turned it upside down to put our clothes on.

"I'm gonna be Marilyn Monroe and Jackie Kennedy. Who are you going to be?" Lee asked me.

"I gonna be Rosa Parks," I said proudly.

Lee looked puzzled. "Who is that?" she wanted to know.

"You will see. You go first. I ain't shore who Mary Monroe be, either."

Lee opened her bag and pulled out a white halter dress of her mothers and I helped her pull it over her clothes. She pushed up her sleeves and put on long white gloves that didn't really go with that halter dress, but I ain't no fashion expert. Then she pulled out a yellow scarf and told me to pretend it was a blonde wig. She tied it around her face and stroked the ends like she was stroking her hair and doing something funny with her lips. Looked like she was making fish lips, so I did my lips back at her, and she thought it was so funny.

"So, who is she?" I asked.

"I am the voluptuous movie star, Marilyn Monroe!" Lee said, showing me her sad figure.

"What 'vol-UP-chus' mean? That the name of a movie at the picture show?"

"That means I have a curvy figure in all the right places, according to Daddy," Lee said as she picked up a little twig to use as a fake cigarette. She took a fake puff, tilted her head back and blew up in the air.

"If you is a movie star, you awfully flat chested. Com'ere," I said. I stuffed some of the other clothes she brung up round her bosom area. "Now you are right voluminous... I mean voluptuous!"

She handed me a lip stick tube to put some lips on her... I ain't ever put lipstick on my own self much less anyone else. That was a trick. She puckered up for me and I laughed.

"Naw, do your lips like this here," I said, tightening my lips with my teeth showing. "Close your lips. Not like that! Relax your lips."

Lee had lipstick on her teeth and upper lip and chin, not much on her lips, but I was the onliest one looking, so I said, "Oh baby, you look beautiful! Pink is yo' color!"

"Thank you, darling," Lee said in a real breathy voice. Then in her own voice, she said, "Shine, sit down on the couch and pretend you are the president."

"Which one? The dead one or the one we just got."

"The dead one," Lee said, and she turned around to climb up on the stage.

When she turned around, I was laying down on the couch with my eyes closed.

"Shine, what on earth are you doing?" Lee said, obviously irritated with me.

"Well, you told me to act like I was the dead president!"

"Yes, the dead one, but pretend he is still alive and sit up. Marilyn is gonna sing to you."

"White girl, you is confusing me…"

"I saw this on tv, so pretend you are Mr. Kennedy," she cleared her throat and changed to a real breathy, and I'd even say sexy, adult voice. "Happy Birthday, to you, Happy birthday to you, Happy birthday, Mr. President, Happy Birthday to you!"

"That really happened? Some little sexpot sang to President Kennedy in front of Miss Jackie? Are you kidding me? No Black woman would ever let another Black woman embarrass her like that. She'd kill her for that!"

"Well, a few months after Marilyn Monroe sang that to JFK last year, she *was* found dead."

"See, what'd I tell you."

"Maybe *somebody* did it, but they said it was a drug overdose," Lee said sadly as she changed into her next outfit. "You don't really think someone would kill somebody for singing to their husband do you?"

"Lee, you got a lot to learn, girl. I don't care whether you is black or white, you don't mess with a woman's man. You not that much younger than me, but you ain't too young to learn that."

Lee put on a skirt with a square jacket and added a pillbox hat and I knew right away who that was.

"You is Mrs. Jackie Kennedy!" I said.

"Yes, and I am here to have tea with you, Miss Rosa Parks, so you better get dressed."

While I was dressing Lee added, "I know your birthday is in a couple of weeks, Adeline, so I brought you something. But don't open it until then!"

"Aww! Gimme a hint!"

"Well, it's something you can read and something you can eat," Lee hinted. "And that is all I am going to say. One time my daddy took me with him to get a gift for my mama for Christmas and he told me not to tell her what it was because it was a surprise. I reckon I was around three or four. He got her a waffle iron. I didn't know what that was, but I knew what an iron was. So, I asked Mama if she wanted me to give her a hint and she did. I said it was something you iron with. Ha! She was mad for a month, thinking Daddy got her an iron. She had gotten five of those when she got married. She was so mad and then so surprised when she opened it up and it was something to make waffles with!"

"What is waffles?" I asked. "Is that what you brung me to eat for my birthday?"

"No, I got you something sweeter than that. Waffles are like crunchy pancakes or a flapjack with a grid on it. It holds the syrup in the little holes on the grid. "

I stood there wondering why people bother with gifts like that when they can just make flapjacks and save they money. I had on my pill box hat with netting over my eyes, my mother's gloves, a long Sunday coat hiding my clothes and an old pair of round eyeglasses from one of my grandparents. I pulled my hair back in a bun under my hat like I had seen of Miss Parks in pictures.

Lee changed her voice again, not so sexy this time but sugary sweet. "I am so glad you came to have tea with me Mrs. Parks. Come in and have a seat. We have delicious bologna sandwiches and peanut butter and banana sandwiches. Here is a bite of each and oh my, how are we going to split our drink?"

"What's the matter, you don't wanna drink after me?" I asked as I took a bite of my sandwich and stared at her.

"Can't you take a sip, then I take a sip? I will wipe it off real good."

"No... and it's not because you are black. It's because of microbes. I can't drink after white or Black people. You shouldn't either. You just drink that one, I will get more at home later."

"You are making it up. Just go ahead and say it.... it's because I am Black."

"No really, I don't want anybody's germs."

I took a long swig of the Pepsi and set it forcefully on the milk crate, in front of Lee. I stared at her as she took a bite of her sandwich, and then another bite. I kept staring. I was Rosa Parks.

"Who done told you not to drink after Negroes?" I said boldly.

"Nobody. I drink after Trey and Pam, and sometimes Barbara Jane, but Mama told me not to drink after anybody at school." Lee said with her head down not looking me in the eye.

"Well, this ain't school. Besides, ain't I as good as your sister?" I said very softly. "That acid in that drink probably kilt ever germ in it."

Lee stared at me as she raised the bottle to her lips and took a sip. I ain't so sure the bottle actually touched her lips in the first swig, but it did later when she learnt the first one ain't killing her. I remembered I had a packet of peanuts Mr. Alvie had given me, so we put that in our Pepsi. Lee and I always added that to our Pepsi Colas...one more thing we had in common.

"Now, Mrs. Kennedy, tell me about how you made these delicious sandwiches," I said a little more sweetly, smiling at her. She say she heared that was Mr. Elvis' favorite: Put mayo on one slice of bread, peanut butter on the other slice, then cut yourself a half of banana on top and sprinkle it with some sugar. Mmm, that's some good eating, right there.

After we finished eating, I said, "Now you got to pretend this couch is a bus so I can tell you who Rosa Parks is. Pretend I am sitting on the front of the bus and ain't no seats left."

"Oh, Miss Rosa, white people aren't allowed to ride on black peoples' buses." Lee said, still talking like Mrs. Kennedy.

"No dear heart, you got it all wrong. Black people ain't allowed to ride on white people's buses, not the other way around. So, you pretend this be a community bus with both white and black, and the bus be full, and you come in and tell me to move so you can sit down."

Lee nodded her head like she got it and said, "Hi, Mrs. Parks, how are you today? I don't see any more seats on the bus. Is there any more room on your seat if you slide over?"

"Ain't no white man or woman gonna squeeze in with a black woman! Is you crazy?"

"Well, how am I supposed to know that. Jackie Kennedy rides around in a limo not a bus and I only ride the school bus to school with white children, not a daggum grown black woman!"

"Try it again, but act like you is a man," I instructed.

Lee was still dressed like Mrs. Kennedy, still with pink lipstick all over her face, but she deepened her voice. "Howdy, Ma'am. Did you see the sign on this here bus? It says, 'Colored Seated in the Rear'," she said it with authority, putting her hands on her hips and trying to look manly.

I snickered, not because of what she was saying, but because she looked ridiculous with that lipstick and dress on, trying to act like a man. I tried to get ahold of myself and said, "Ain't no more seats back there, sir."

"I guess one of us is out of luck, but since you are a woman..."

"Just let me tell you who she is... that ain't how it happened. You don't have a clue what it's like to be Black.

74

My lord. Sit down, girl. Yes, that sign say, 'Colored Seated in the Rear,' 'Colored Seated in the Rear,' '*Colored Seated in the Rear!*'" I got louder and louder, pointing at a faked sign in the air.

With that, I climbed up on our playhouse "stage" and started talking.

"I am Rosa Parks from Alabama. In 1955, I got on a community bus after work and sat down. Pretty shortly, all the seats were taken. A white man got on the bus, and the bus driver asked me and the other black people to stand up to ride. I refused to stand up for a man. I was tired of being treated like second-class. The bus driver called the police on me and had me arrested! I was charged with breaking a segregation law and told to pay a $10. I told them I ain't gonna pay it," Shine said, shaking her hand. "I won't guilty, and the law was illegal. I took it to a higher court. Dr. Martin Luther King helped me, and all the Black people boycott all the buses in Montgomery, Alabama. That won't easy since not many of us had cars and we depended on the buses to get to work, but we did it. Our boycott lasted for over a year. My case went all the way to the Supreme Court! They ruled that segregation laws in Alabama was against the constitution of the United States. But as of right now, nothing much has changed. Least not in Bishopville. It still be 'Colored Seated in the Rear'."

Then Lee said, "So, this woman you all dressed up to be is just an old black woman on a bus that wouldn't let someone have her seat? I never heard of her. She isn't that famous, 'specially if nothing changed. What did you dress up like her for?"

For a good three minutes I just stared at her. I wanted to smack her. I stood there, breathing heavy, and it was ever thing I could do to keep from telling her she won't my friend anymore. I thought, 'what would my mama do?'

I got off the stage and hugged Lee with tears in my eyes and said, "Dear heart, if you don't remember any conversation you and I ever have, I want you to remember this one when you are older. Even if you don't understand, and someday I pray, Lord I pray, you do, I forgive you and I love you."

On my birthday a few days later, I opened the bag Lee gave me that day. Inside was a school picture with a note saying to put it on my bedroom wall with the drawing so I would have some "family" photos on my wall. It also contained a Butternut candy bar, a potholder Lee made her own self, and a picture she drew of us. Underneath my picture, Lee wrote, "my bestest friend".

CHAPTER NINE

~Lee~8 yrs old/1964

"The thing that is worse than rebellion is the thing that causes rebellion."

Frederick Douglas

As 1963 turned into 1964, rebellion was abounding. Rock and Roll music was on the scene with rebellious teenagers loving the Beatles and the Beach Boys, gyrating their bodies like Elvis. The Jitter Bug of the '50s was replaced with the Shag and the Swing to the Motown beats of the Temptations, The Supremes, and the Drifters. Race riots arose in many major cities all through the year with Afro-Americans who were tired of being second-class citizens. And I was doing a little rebelling at home myself.

That February our garage was renovated into a new family room, and we got a large console television just in time to watch the Ed Sullivan show broadcast the Beatles. Even my mother loved the Beatles! Over the next few years, she taught us the words to many of their songs and we performed for company. One particularly memorable performance was when the Davis family and the Gardener family came to play cards one night. Collins Gardner, Robbie Davis and Trey were the Beatles. Back then, almost all little boys wore buzz cuts, not long hair. So, they tied handkerchiefs in a knot at each corner and laid them over their heads. Pam and I had just gotten white boots for Christmas. We donned them to pretend we were the boys backup singers and Go-go Girls, neither of which the Beatles really had. Trey fell on our brick hearth and had to be rushed to the hospital for stitches. Once again, I was traumatized at the thought of a sibling not coming home from the hospital.

That spring, the daffodils bloomed, I got another bunny cake, and turned eight. I got my first Nancy Drew mystery books as a birthday gift and instantly became hooked. I loved reading and would hide in the bathroom adjacent to my bedroom to get out of chores and read. I was allergic to dust, Clorox, and many soaps and detergents…and housework. That would probably would have gotten me in more trouble than it did, but Lizzie was in on it. She knew I lined the bathtub with blankets, took a pillow in and locked the door. She knew where to find me if my mother missed me for long. Lizzie would knock on the door and say, "Lee, you in there? I believe yo' time is up!"

Pam was usually outside playing with the animals, but I was allergic to many of them, too, especially kitty cats. I thought cats were beautiful, but I was forbidden to play with them because my eyes would swell shut. Lizzie knew I loved them, When I came inside, she'd say, "Go wash yo hands, and I'll fix an ice pack for your eyes 'fore your mama sees you."

I am not sure why Lizzie covered for me like that, but as far as cleaning, she would probably rather do the work herself than have me do it half right and have to go behind me to do it over again. Lizzie and I were very close. I would discuss things with her about boys or my body or about life in general that I would not dare ask my mother.

One day I asked Lizzie, "Where do you go to the bathroom when you are working at our house since we don't have a sign saying which bathroom is the 'colored' one?"

"I go outside."

"*What?* Mama doesn't let you use our bathrooms?"

"It's all right, chile. I used to it."

"No, it's not all right, Lizzie!" I said, disgusted. "From now on you can go in my bathroom off my bedroom, OK?"

"You sure?"

"Yeah, I will cover for you like you cover for me, if I need to.

Not long after that, Mama saw Lizzie coming out of my bathroom, smoothing down her apron and heard the commode flush.

"Lizzie, did you just use that bathroom?" she asked sharply.

"Yessum, Lee said it be all right..."

"Well, did you clean it?"

"Mama!" I said, shocked.

"Well, if she is going to use your bathroom, she needs to sanitize it each time. Lee, go get the Lysol and the Comet and the toilet brush."

I hurried out of the room. I could hear the disgust in her voice, and I was confused. When I came back to my room, Mama was gone, and Lizzie was sitting on the tub.

"I am so sorry, Lizzie. I really don't mind if you use my bathroom. What did she say while I went to get this?"

"She say, 'Don't use the front bathroom—it be for company'."

I sprayed the seat and wiped it off and hugged Lizzie. "I'll be sure to sanitize it for you when I use it, too, Lizzie."

Lizzie kept us after school a lot while she was doing housework. One day Trey wanted to try her snuff. She told him she would make a special batch for us. She mixed sugar and cocoa in cups and gave one to each of us. We would put about a half teaspoon in our bottom lip and act like we were dipping snuff. It was fun until Trey started spitting it on us. He soon decided he wanted to try real cigarettes. He got behind Mom and Dad's bed, rolled up some paper, and put in some of Lizzie's loose tobacco. After about three puffs, Trey triggered his asthma and after about six, he dropped the fast burning, hand-rolled cigarette and started a fire! Pam and I yelled for Lizzie, and she quickly got the fire under control. Bless her heart, she never did tell Mama about all she had to put up with taking care of us. We knew our secrets were safe with her.

Mama had a rule in the house that the family had to all eat at the kitchen table together when Daddy was home. Lizzie was allowed to eat when we ate, but she always took her plate to the family room and ate by herself. One day I had something I wanted to discuss with Lizzie. I was mad at my parents about something involving blaming me for something I did not do, yet again. I quietly made my plate and went to the family room with Lizzie, hoping no one would notice. However, Daddy started calling me to the table. I yelled back, "I am eating with Lizzie."

"That's not your place. Your place is at the table with us."

"I want to eat with Lizzie today, please."

"I said to come take your place with the family at the table NOW!" my dad yelled back.

I paused for a minute and drew in a deep breath. "No, thank you. I am going to eating with Lizzie in the family room unless she is allowed to eat with us at the kitchen table."

Daddy came to the door. His face was red, and he was still chewing his last bite of food as he talked, "Young lady, if you don't come to the table in two minutes, you are getting a belt."

I stared at him. He left the room. Lizzie said, "Lee, you best mind your Daddy. You know he'll use that belt."

"I am eating with you unless they let you eat at the table."

"Shug, they ain't gonna let the help eat at the table. You go on in there."

"No, I haven't finished talking to you.

"It ain't worth getting a whipping over."

"Maybe it will make him think about how stupid my whippings are. Besides, black people should be able to eat at the same table as white people."

"That ain't the way it is."

All of the sudden my right arm was jerked up. Lizzie grabbed my plate just before my food flew off the plate. Right in front of Lizzie I got about five lashes with Daddy's leather belt.

Afterwards I said defiantly, "Since you have already spanked me for it, I am *not* going to the table. You need to think about what you just did."

Daddy was shaking his head at me as he said, "What? You need to apologize to me before you get another whipping, young lady."

"I am sorry I disappointed you, but I did what I believe was right. I always do what I believe is right. That's what you taught me and what we're taught at church. You need to apologize to Lizzie," I told him boldly. He stomped off.

The next time I remember eating lunch with Lizzie was at the end of the school year to

discuss something I heard at school. President Johnson was about to pass the Civil Rights Act of 1964. It would make segregation illegal and give everyone the right to vote. I wanted to know what Lizzie thought about it. In my eight-year-old mind, all it meant to me was that Daddy couldn't keep Lizzie from eating at our table, and I was so excited.

"You better get back to the kitchen. Mr. Vern gonna be after you in a minute, you know."

"I don't care. I have something to talk to you about. Have you ever voted?"

Lizzie held her hand with her biscuit in it over her mouth and laughed. "No chile, ain't no Black people in 'Merica been voting. Most of us can't read or write."

"You can. Don't they let you vote?"

"No, baby. What they teaching you in school?"

"That's why I want to talk to you. President Johnson is trying to make it so Black people can eat at the table with us and can use our bathrooms and can vote!"

About the time we both saw my daddy move back from the door and stood in the shadow of the doorway.

"Ain't nothing gonna change in the South, baby. Ain't nothing gonna change," Lizzie said.

But she elbowed me, winked and smiled. I smiled back. And on July 2nd Congress passed LBJ's Civil Rights Act of 1964 into being, making it illegal to discriminate against anyone based on race, religion, origin, or sexual orientation. Lizzie was right. It took the South a long time to embrace it.

That summer we were swimming in the pool down at the farm, the baptismal pool that my grandfather let the black minister build, several times a week. The pool was icy cold from the artesian water and the smell of manure permeated the air since the dairy was so close. We kids quickly got used to both, as usual. My mother had put a huge watermelon in the artesian spring to get cold. That day Shine and Peggy and a few other black children showed up and watched us swim from a distance at the fence. I got out of the water after a while and asked, "Mom, can we cut the watermelon now?"

"Sure," my mother said, shielding her eyes from the sun to talk to me.

"Since it's so big, can we share it with Shine and her friends?"

She frowned at me and let out a sigh.

"The Civil Rights Act says we have to," I said with my hands on my hips.

"Well, OK, then!" she laughed.

We all dried off and hurried over the tobacco shed across the dirt road from the pool with Shine and her friends. Mama put newspapers down and cut the watermelon, singing the song she always sang us before we had watermelon:

Just plant a watermelon at the head of my grave and let the juice... run through.

Just plant a watermelon at the head of my grave, that's all I ask of you.

Now the chicken and the 'possum are all mighty fine,
But there ain't nothing like that watermelon vine!
So, plant a watermelon at the head of my grave, and
let the juice... run through!

The rest of the summer and fall of that year and the next was filled with fun parties for teenagers on our back porch. Our family hosted an exchange student each year for the summer. In the past, we'd had someone from Greece and Ecuador and the next two were from Austria and Mexico. The parties with home-churned ice cream or grilling hamburgers out back always included playing Mama's 45 records of the Beatles and Beach music. The prettiest girls in the community and the boys from our church were always there and they didn't seem to mind teaching us little kids how to dance to the music or to us being around. "I want to Hold Your Hand," "Twist and Shout," and "She Loves Me" were played over and over so loud that Lizzie said she could hear them all the way to her house a mile down the road! I loved beach music just as much, and my favorite was "Under the Boardwalk," and "You've Lost that Loving Feeling," although I had no idea the meaning of the words. The Austrian and the Mexican sure loved the music and the girls! The Austrian taught us to squeeze the grapes that grew in our front yard with our bare feet and make wine. The Mexican proposed to every single woman at the parties and wrecked three of my father's tractors before he was sent home. After that, I don't think we had any more exchange students.

For Christmas that year, Pam and I got more Barbies and a Skipper, and Trey got a G.I. Joe and military-related toys. The Viet Nam war was escalating so I guess even toy manufacturers were in on the propaganda. Trey played with us more after he got his G.I. Joe, but we had to play army with him in return. While we made clothes for our dolls, Trey sewed tents and stretchers for his soldier.

At the end of the year, Daddy signed a contract with Fort Jackson to rent the land behind our house for soldiers to do field training exercises. He said the swamp back there was an excellent training ground to simulate rice paddies and that we would not be able to go in the woods next summer. I could not believe it! That was where our playhouse was!

"Daddy, you own that land?" I asked

"Yes, all the way back to the swamp and back on this side to the other side of the hayfield.

Why?" Daddy looked at me quizzically.

"Well, I thought people just dumped trash back there, and I've already homesteaded it."

My dad snickered. "Where did you hear a word like that?"

"School."

"So, you have homesteaded it, huh? I don't think you need to put a home on it because you live here with us, don't you."

"I have a playhouse back there."

"Well, the truth is I already own it so you can't homestead it."

"Hmm, can I buy my part then?"

"Do you have any money?"

"No, but I can work in tobacco or something for you.'"

Daddy thought for a minute. "I tell you what. I will let you register cows for me, and you can have that little spot that has moss on it back there. Is that a deal?"

"Ok, how do you register cows?

"You just draw the spots or marking on each cow on a registration paper. You are good at drawing. You can do that."

"And you will tell the Army not to bother my land when they are back there"

"I will tell them not to mess with your playhouse."

"Shake on it," I said, not realizing he got the best end of that deal.

CHAPTER TEN

~Adeline~1965

"You know your children are growing up when they stop asking where they came from and refuse to tell you where they are going."

P.J. O' Rourke

We didn't have no money to go up town to the movie theater, but we did go over to the Newsom farm sometimes at dusk and they be showing a picture show on a big old sheet for a nickel. Lee was always talking about going to movies with her little white friend Jackie and wanted to know why the white peoples had to sit on the bottom seats and the black peoples gots to sit on the top ones. She said she wanted to sit in that balcony because she thought they was the best seats in the house. When Peggy's birthday came round, she talked me into surprising Peggy with a trip to the picture show in the Bishopville. She said she had done some work for her daddy and had enough money to pay my way and Peggy's

85

way into the show too, but she and Jackie wanted to sit upstairs in the balcony with us.

I askt her, "How you gonna do that when you ain't Black?"

"Jackie and I can wear toboggans and mittens and black leggings or pants," she said.

"What about your white face? You ain't even a bit tanned!

"You got any black shoe polish?"

"Girl, you can't put shoe polish on your face—that ain't what we look like!"

"Well, what can we use that is brown and will come off easier? How about make-up? You have any dark make-up?"

"Naw."

"I'll think of something. You and Peggy just meet us in Bishopville in front of the theater at 1:00 Saturday. Jackie's sister is going to drop us off."

So, Sat'day come around and we be there. Elvis Presley was playing in Blue Hawaii. That probably the only way we ever gonna get to Hawaii! Lee and Jackie showed up and they is still white.

So, I say, "You can't figure out how to turn yourselves black, can you?"

"Ssshh! Come over here!" Lee says to me and pulls me over against the next building away from everyone standing in line. She pulled out a little compact and started putting dark makeup on Jackie while Peggy and I stood huddled around them. She looked pretty good 'sept her nose and mouth be shiny. Then we watch Jackie do up Lee.

"Do her ears and her neck," I said. "And pull your collar up."

We go pay for our tickets and head up the steps to the balcony by the sign that said "Colored" with an arrow pointing up.

"Hey! Hey you!"

We pushed Lee and Jackie ahead of us and I glanced back. Carl Watts, the manager of the theater was after a black boy headed into the white part of the theater, not after us. We went on up and got our seats, and the smell of buttery popcorn and old theater crud filled our nostrils as we settled in. None of us had money for popcorn or soda pop, but I was just glad to be there. The cartoons had just finished, and the movie was about to start when Mr. Carl came by with his flashlight and shined it right in Lee's eyes.

"You girls all right up here?"

Lee froze, so I spoke for her, "Yessuh."

"It ain't Halloween, so why you gals dressed like this?"

Lee finally spoke up, "We just wanted to sit with our friends to watch the movie."

"You best be sitting down there with your people—I know your mama and daddy."

Mr. Watts lowered his flashlight, and I could see Lee squirming in her seat with the reflection of the movie on her face as she answered, "Would it be better for us to sit up here, or these two girls sit down there with us?"

"Girl, you better get your butt downstairs where you belong."

"You know about the Civil Rights Act that got passed last year, right?" Lee boldly whispered back to him.

"Girl, how old are you?" Mr. Watts asked.

"I am about to turn nine," Lee said as the show is about to start.

"Did your Daddy tell you to say that?"

Jackie spoke up, "No, he didn't. He don't even know we are here!"

Mr. Carl shook his head and kind of chuckled. "Lee, you're just like your daddy. I will keep my eye on you girls, but don't ever pull this stunt again, you hear?"

As soon as he left, we all giggled, and so did everyone around us. They didn't look much like blacks, but they sho thought they'd pass. Ever body around us knew they won't doing black face like minstrels to make fun of us. They knew those girls wanted to sit with us, even Mr. Carl, so nobody had a problem with what they done did. The blacks in the balcony pretty much ignored them and did what they usually done during the movie—used their straws to shoot paper napkin spitballs down to the first floor. The movie "Blue Hawaii" was real good. We got to see Hawaii, and we got to see Elvis sing and dance. And Lee and Jackie sweared they was both going to marry him when they growed up. We all got a big kick out of that.

The girls went to the bathroom and tried to wash off their faces before Jackie's sister picked them up, but you could see they had been up to something. I ain't sure how they ever got that mess off their faces. Turns out that little round compact of brown stuff they be rubbing all over their faces was brown boot polish. Lee told me later she got a whipping for going up to the balcony and using Vern's boot polish. I felt so bad about it. I don't know why that got her a whipping, but Mr. Vern told her it won't safe for a white girl to be up there in that balcony. Heck, it was less safe for a black girl to be by herself in the white part the way things was.

But change was coming. Shortly after that Rev. Martin Luther King, Jr. led the first march from Selma to Montgomery, Alabama. He led what was supposed to be a peaceful march to protest lack of voting rights for blacks and other racial messes. But the Alabama state troopers used whips and nightsticks and teargas on those marchers, and it became chaos. In the end, though, it was all worth it because the Voters Rights Act of 1965 was signed and passed by President Johnson before the end of the year.

Lee told me that Vern rented the woods and the field beside their house to the army that summer, and we couldn't go back there in the woods that year. We decided we'd just have to go to the other side of the road or to the other side of the house. Since we didn't have our playhouse in the woods, we'd just take a transistor radio out with us and sing and dance and be go-go girls. On one side of the house was a clay pit where we pretended it was beach sand, and we danced to beach music or the likes of James Brown and the Beatles. We would stick branches in the sand pit, standing them up like microphones and pretend we was the Supremes. I told Lee she best not put no more boot polish on her face. Some days it was just me and Lee, and some days Puddin and Moonpie joined us, and sometimes Lee had some white friends that showed up. But it was always me and Lee, the leaders of the pack.

One day Lee saw me digging up worms with a scoop in the cow pasture down at the farm and askt me what I was gonna do with all my worms. That be the best place to find worms and slugs, in daggum fields with cow manure in it. I told her I was playing hooky from school the next day to go fishing cuz my daddy ain't been feeding us. He ain't been gardening no more, ain't been taken care of nothing. I knew I could catch me some fish to eat. Lee decided to she gonna play hooky from school and go with me. I don't remember exactly why she didn't want to go to school or why I won't going, but I knew I was going fishing down at Lynches River. So, we came up with a plan. I really wanted her to go cuz I hated putting those daggum worms on that hook by myself. After the school bus picked her up, they always stopped down at the farm to pick up Barbara Jane. She was going to hand a note to the bus driver that she was getting off to go see her daddy at the dairy barn. Pam and Al were home with mumps or measles or something that Lee had already done had. Then she gwine meet me at the barn, and I would have the bait and the poles, and we'd head out down the dirt road to the river after the bus be gone. Ever thing worked as planned til we got 'bout halfway down that dirt road. I had them poles over my shoulder, and Lee was walking behind me, carrying the worms.

"Shine, you always catch more fish than me. What's your secret?"

"Getting someone else to bait the hook for me," I said.

I could hear Lee giggling behind me. "I'll bait your hook for you. Worms don't bother me. Daddy Mac says the reason I don't catch as much as everybody else is I don't know how to hold my mouth right. What does that mean?"

I thought for a minute.

"It could mean you ain't smiling. You ever noticed how he always be smiling?" I turned around and grinned at her, "Let's sing. Maybe the fish will hear us coming and come up to see if we brought them some food."

We started singing as usual, "This Land is Your Land, This Land is My Land."

This land is your land, this land is my land,
From California to the New York Island,
From the redwood forest to the gulf stream waters,
This land was made for you and me.

As I was walking that ribbon of highway,
I saw above me that endless skyway;
I saw before me that golden valley,
This land was made for you and me.
I've roamed and rambled and followed my footsteps,
To the sparkling sands of her diamond deserts,
And all around me a voice was sounding,
This land was made for you and me.

This Woody Guthrie song was taught in all the schools so we both knew it, at least the first few verses. We was having a good ol' time. Then all the sudden, one of them fishing pole lines came loose and was swinging behind me, and the fishhook caught Lee in the lip! It caught her top lip real good, just like she was a big ol' fish! The hook went clear through her lip, and she started squealing like a little pig dropped in bacon grease!

I grabbed the line, then sets down the pole and said, "Be real still and let me see. Oh, lawd. Baby, oh dear heart. If I pull that hook out, it gonna rip your lip apart."

"You can't just pull it out?" Lee asked.

"No chile, it has a barb on it." I said. I drew a picture of it in the sand so she could see what I was talking about. The barb was in the reverse direction of the hook. Either way I would have pulled, that hook was gonna pull her lip.

"I think we need to get Mr. Alvie or your daddy to take a look at this."

"No, I'm supposed to be in school. See if you can get it out. Besides, we've already walked about two miles, haven't we?"

"Yeah, we almost to the river. Let me see what I can do."

'Bout that time, here come Mr. Alvie in his truck with his two little rat terriers riding on his sideboard. He had fishing poles in the back of his truck!

"Well, Shine, looks like you caught a big one! Sweetpea, let me see if I can get that thing out of your lip. Does it hurt?"

"Not really. But it's starting to swell."

Mr. Alvie started whistling through his teeth and smiling while he worked on Lee's lip. He was always whistling, but not the normal way.

"Is you going fishing, Mr. Alvie?" I asked.

"Yeah, I thought you girls might need some company...and some drinks...and a cooler for all those fish you're going to catch," Mr. Alvie chuckled as he worked on Lee.

I couldn't watch so I played with the dogs, Happy and Felix. Mr. Alvie took them ever where he went. He never went fast in his pickup truck cuz they was always on his sideboards.

"I forgot to bring my lunch," I said.

"Don't worry. I have sardines and saltine crackers and maybe some cheese. I always have that for the field hands,

you know. There, I got out the hook! Let's rinse out your mouth real good with some water."

Lee's lip was swollen up twice its size.

"Your nickname for the day is 'Fish Lips'!" I laughed and handed her the bottle of water.

Mr. Alvie put us up in the back of his truck and drove on down to the river with us. He fished with us for most of the day. He caught six fish, I caught five and Lee caught three. We had a good mess of catfish, bluegill and bass. After we got back to the big house, Mr. Alvie helped us dress the fish and he put them back in the cooler on ice. Nobody said anything about we 'sposed to be in school, til Lee spoke up 'bout them fish. Mr. Alvie wanted to split them 'tween the two of us, and Lee won't having it.

"Daddy Mac, I can't take any fish home. I was supposed to be in school today! I was fishing to help Shine out." Lee confessed.

"Well, it's ok to give the fish to Little Miss Sunshine, but it's about time for the school bus to be at your house. If you don't get off the bus, your mama will be worried."

"That's ok I was going to call her and tell her I got off at the farm to register cows. I already told her I was going to do that because that part was the truth."

Mr. Alvie proceeded to give Lee a lecture about honesty and wondered how she gonna explain her big ol' fish lips. He didn't want her to lie about nothing, but she was afraid of Vern's belt, and he knew it.

"Shine, what else you need, shug? How about some pecans and butterbeans and honey? You and Lee go pick up some pecans out there in the yard, and I'll go in the smokehouse and see if I can find some smoked ham to send home with you."

"Thank you, Mr. Alvie," I said.

"Farming hasn't been so great this year. Let your daddy know I'll help him out all I can."

"Thank you, Mr. Alvie, I 'preciate it," I said. "Daddy ain't been the same since Mama died. Ain't really got nothing to do with farming."

"I know, shug, but your daddy lives to farm. The weather for '66 just isn't cooperating."

While we picked up pecans, I askt Lee if she was taught the rest of "This Land is Your Land." Now I know Woody Guthrie wrote that song in 1958 protesting social injustice. In the '60's one of my teachers taught it to me, but Lee had never heard it:

As I went walking, I saw a sign there,
And on the sign, it said "No Trespassing,"
But on the other side it didn't say nothing.
That side was made for you and me.
In the shadow of the steeple, I saw my people,
By the relief office I seen my people;
As they stood there hungry, I stood there asking
Is this land made for you and me?

I just couldn't get it off my mind. Rev. Martin Luther King, Jr. had been marching all over the country for our rights. He was walking that freedom highway.

Nobody can ever stop me,
As I go walking that freedom highway
Nobody living can ever make me turn back
This land was made for you and me.

CHAPTER ELEVEN

~Lee~9 yrs. Old/ 4th grade/1965-6

"Prejudice is a house-plant which is very apt to wilt if you take it out of doors among folks."

H.W. Shaw

The fall of 1965 I started 4th grade with my all-time favorite teacher, Mrs. Betty Colclough.
I adored her, and so did everyone else. I started to really enjoy reading and writing and was developing more relationships with white friends.

While I started accepting that white adults seemed to have a superior feeling toward black people, I was beginning to feel a sense of superiority myself toward impoverished white people. Even black people called them "red necks" and seemed to feel different toward them. I remember one event in Mrs. Colclough's class when I realized this, and it hurt.
The fourth grade had four classrooms and in each room every child had made a mailbox to receive valentines on Valentine's Day. For weeks I could not wait to put my

valentine in one little boy's box, and I didn't even know his name. All I knew from passing him in the hall is that he looked just like a miniature version of Dr. Kildare, a doctor on a popular TV show, and I was smitten. His hair was slicked back with Dippity Do (yes, we really called it that), not in a buzz cut like the other boys. His shirt was always pressed neat and tucked in, and he always had a smile on his tanned face. Mrs. Colclough found out from his teacher what his name was so I could put a valentine in his box. I was thrilled! The next day I saw him getting water at the water fountain. I shyly said, "Did you get the card from "Lee"? That was me!"

When he turned around, grinning, and, front tooth missing, and said in the most redneck voice, "That was from you? I am sure glad that prissy card ain't from no boy! Thank you! Your name had me fooled. Hot Diggity! I can't believe I got myself a girlfriend!"

I recoiled. I was glad no one was around to hear that. As he walked off, I noticed his pants were now too short for his long legs. I was heartbroken. My puppy love crush had ended as fast as it had started. I spent the rest of the year avoiding him. His redneck accent, mannerisms, and ill-fitting clothes had turned me totally off. The incident and feeling reminded me for years that how I present my Southern self may not be or appear as I intend despite my best efforts when prejudice is involved. Ironically, I eventually married a good old boy from Bishopville that had that same thick Southern accent! I eventually learned to value a person's soul.

By the mid-Sixties, the Viet Nam war was escalating, and daily updates filled our news reports. The number of troops doubled over the course of the year, so certainly some of the trainees from Fort Jackson that trained in our back yard that year were sent straight to the front. We could hear them running through the woods, shooting blanks, detonating fake bombs, and yelling at each other when they had a training exercise. Mama would let me take water to them in Mason jars when they came close to the edge of our yard. Of course, I took that opportunity to tell them about the playhouse with strict instructions not to bomb it under any circumstances. By the summer, they made a point to come to the yard to fill their canteens and bring us candy, spent bullets, and other trinkets they could spare. My mother tried to come out to put a stop to us "bothering them," but they would whistle at her, and she finally gave up. Their attention eased the pain of not seeing my friends in the woods as much.

Some of the boys from our church started volunteering for the war. I think the draft came a few years later. One of the guys that enlisted had frequently invited me to go to drive-in movies on dates as his little sister. He didn't have a sister and the girls' mothers would not let the girls go without a chaperone. I am not sure how great I did at being a chaperone, as I was put in the front seat with all the popcorn and candy I could possibly eat, with my eyes glued on the movie. My mother always had to approve of the movie choice, but she let me go. She adored Randy. Before long he enlisted to go to Viet Nam.

Another guy that got drafted, one of the Galloway boys, asked Daddy if I could take care of his horse while he was gone to Nam. When he came back, Freckles and I had bonded, and were doing horse shows. Freckles would not have anything to do with him, so he decided to give the horse to me. I had that horse until I went to college. Before the first guy left for Viet Nam, he would occasionally ride the trails in the woods with me with a horse I assume was from the Galloways, too, where Freckles had come from or from David Lucas's, my bus driver. David also rode horses with us sometimes.

I particularly liked to ride Freckles down at the farm. She could gallop full throttle down the dirt roads, jump ditches and trot down with me to the tobacco barn if I wanted to work. One day Daddy Mac had helped me put the saddle on

Freckles and something was wrong with the girth. Neither of us could get it to tighten properly, but finally Daddy Mac thought he had on. I got on Freckles and galloped down the dirt road in front of the farmhouse as he watched me jump several ditches. Then I turned around at the end of the road to come back, and Freckles galloped back toward the barn. Just as she came full speed, she spotted a rattle snake coiled in the road and went berserk. She bucked and bucked, then bolted toward the barn at the fastest speed I'd ever seen her go. I desperately held on to the horn, her mane, and the rein. All of the sudden, the girth gave loose, and I was under her belly in a flash! Her hooves were hitting my head! I could hear Daddy Mac and Shine yelling at me to hold my feet tight around her. My feet were still in the stirrups, and I was hanging on for dear life. I knew if I let go, she would trample me. On the other hand, I was afraid her hooves were going to knock me out. Much to my relief, Daddy Mac and Shine were able to stop Freckles at the barn and get me from under the horse safely. I had to walk her down the dirt road to the tobacco barn several times before she would let me ride her again because she kept shying away from the dirt road as soon as we would get to the turn where she saw the rattlesnake.

Daddy Mac seemed to think me riding under the belly of a horse was as funny as when I first shot a rifle with him. He sat me up next to a pine tree to shoot the rifle before I went hunting with him. The kick of that rifle knocked me out when my head hit the tree, and I woke up to Daddy Mac chuckling. Shine said, "Mr. Alvie, you sure do seem to delight in seeing yo' grandchildren half kill they selves." And he just chuckled at that, and said, "Well, we come from strong stock."

My mother seemed to be getting more lenient about me going up town to the theater alone with my white friend, Jackie. We went almost every Saturday to the movie theater, mostly to see Elvis Presley movies. I still could not understand why black people were not allowed to sit among us while we worked beside them at the farm. And even more puzzling to me was why my black friends were not at school with me when I was hearing more and more on television about how schools were supposed to be integrated.

That summer Daddy Mac volunteered to take the little girls in the family, Bobbie, Pam and me, to Edisto with him to clean the ALCEMAC, his summer beach house at Edisto Island, SC. We could each take one friend, so I asked him if Shine could go. He said, "We'll see." But when we got to the farm to go, Shine wasn't there. Instead, Pecan was there, an underprivileged white girl who also worked on the farm. She was closer to Bobbie's age, but I knew her.

"Where is Shine?" I asked Daddy Mac.

"Shine can't go this time, Blondie. They can't do without her on the farm." Daddy Mac said.

"Why couldn't Pecan work in her place?" I asked my grandfather as he walked away.

"You know why she couldn't go, and Colin wouldn't let her anyway because she doesn't know how to swim," my grandfather argued.

"I could teach her. I should have been able to pick the friend I wanted." I pouted.

In the fall of 1966, I was supposed to go to public school and enter the 5th grade. However, the federal government said it would no longer help fund schools that remained segregated, and in the eleven years since the Supreme Court passed the Brown vs. The Board of Education ruling that schools should be integrated not segregated, nothing had changed in our county. Part of the problem was that our county was 85% black, and most of those were either illiterate or poorly educated. It would be hard to find teachers educated well enough to teach the white kids. The majority were still field hands who attended classes sporadically like Shine or never finished school like her father. While federal aid had been given to assist teaching blacks in those eleven years, the students still had not shown up consistently, and most of their teachers were not well-taught themselves. The few teachers that had graduated were not up to the level of teaching white people were accustomed back then, and white parents were not willing to put their educated white children in school with blacks that were several years behind. The white people in our county got together and started a private school and thumbed their nose at the government. The federal government refused to accredit our school, fund it, or recognize it in any way. Meanwhile, the public schools did integrate with people that could not afford the private school, and it took a generation later before we saw any real changes in South Carolina. By then, I felt very strongly that children, my son included, should go to public school not to support the government, but to learn to interact with all races.

The private school wasn't ready by the time school was ready to start that fall, so we went to school in Bethlehem Methodist Church for the first several months. One advantage to a private school is that you can add religious curriculum. Our board did it and they eventually voted on a name. They named our new school after our county, Robert E. Lee Academy, but the name opened controversy with the Lee County residents. By some accounts, Robert E. Lee was a stern taskmaster of his many inherited; and by others, he was a very lenient and hated the institution of slavery. Evidence shows that his detractors and haters lied about some of Lee's treatment of his slaves and, right or wrong, owning slaves was an accepted practice of that era going back before Biblical times. Nonetheless, in 2020 the board changed the name to just Lee Academy. It is also now integrated and accredited and has come full circle.

I begged Daddy to let me help put in tobacco and pick cotton, and that year he finally relented. He paid me a measly fifty cents a day. I made up the difference. My fine straight hair was sandy brown with sun-bleached blonde streaks in it, much different than all the Afro-American women's hair at the barn. They would pay me a nickel a braid to braid it just so they could feel it. I would go home with a pocket full of nickels and a hair full of braids. Mama would fuss and take them out, and I would return the next day and let them braid it all over again. Minimum wage in 1966 was just $1.25 an hour, and women only made about 59 cents to every dollar a man made. Considering that, I made in an afternoon what the help was making in an hour and that is, only if farmers were required to pay minimum wage.

Still, loved to go the tobacco barn. Not only did I get to see my friend Shine, I also got to do work I liked. My job was to get three good tobacco leaves and hand it off to the stringer. Shine was a top stringer, and she was fast and amazing at it. She let it be known if you were not handing off fast enough to her, you needed to hand off to someone else. She would take three leaves and you could hear the fresh zip quickly up the string on to the tobacco stick which sat on something akin to a carpenter's sawhorse. Then she would tie and zip three leaves up the other side of the stick and repeated this pattern, stringing the stick to and fro until it was full of tobacco. Next, she would call for the runners to run the stick up in the rafters in the tobacco barn. Although we were friends, Shine let me know real quick, she would prefer I hand off to a less experienced stringer. I was too slow for her!

Shine and I played together when we were waiting for the mules to bring a tobacco drag with a load of fresh leaves from the field. A drag was a wooden cart with no wheels that mules drug along the dirt roads between the fields and the barns. Sometimes Daddy Mac let me ride on top of the tobacco leaves to the barn with the first load of the day. Shine and I would play Jacob's ladder or Cat's in the Cradle with our tobacco string or, sometimes, Hopscotch in the dirt. Other times we would all Limbo with tobacco sticks to music from the radio. Music was always either being sung or played at the tobacco barn.

I loved listening to the tobacco help sing Negro spirituals while they worked. Many of the songs had been passed down several generations since slavery. While they were singing, the constant rhythm of the zinging sound from the stringing added a nice backup. The guys up in the rafters would often tap out the rhythm on their wooden sticks in the rafters, and the acoustics in the tobacco barn would reverberate throughout the shed. At least one person was always a hummer and one or more would be an Amen-er. One song that I liked was "Amen" because there were three participants: the head singer, usually a deep-voiced man, the hummers, and the choir answering the man. "Amen" went something like this:

A-men, Oh Lawdy!
A-men, have mercy.
Amen, amen, amen.
Sing it over now.

A-men, Oh Lawdy!
A-men, have mercy.
Amen, amen, amen.

See the little baby
Lying in a manger
On Christmas morning!
Amen, amen, amen.

See Him in a temple
Talking to the elders
How they are marveled.
Amen, amen, amen.

See Him at the seashore,
Preaching to the peoples,
Healing all the sick ones
Amen, amen, amen.

See Him at the garden
Praying to the father
In deepest sorrow
Amen, amen, amen.

See Him on the Cross
Bearing all my sins
In bitter agony
Amen, amen, amen.

Yes, He died to save us
And He rose at Easter!
Now He lives forever.
Amen, amen, amen.

Hallelujah!
Jesus is my Saviour
For He lives forever.
Amen, amen, amen.

I also liked "Nobody Knowed de Trouble I Seen," "Steal Away," and "Mine Eyes Have Seen the Glory." Barbara Jane said she did not like that one because it was the Battle Cry of the Republic. At the time I didn't know what that meant. I said I didn't like it because she didn't like it, but secretly I tapped my foot to it quite a bit. I also noticed Daddy Mac whistled it through his teeth a lot, too.

Not many people went by their real name at the barn. Pam was Peanut (Daddy Mac always called her that) and I was Sweetpea or Blondie. Some of the other names I remember are Noonie Gal, Pie, Peaches, Snookie, Queenie, Dimp (short for Dimples) and Coot. I can only imagine the origin of all those names. Men and women of all ages worked the fields and the barns, from adolescents to grandparents. We discussed all kinds of things. Religion was one thing that was a hot topic. Since I was well-versed in all things biblical going to church every single Sunday and most Wednesday nights, I had to bite my tongue a lot. One conversation I remember was Queenie and Snookie arguing about was how a particular Bible verse was worded. Daddy Mac and I listened nearby as they went back and forth about it for a bit. Finally, Queenie said, "Well, your version might have been in the Old Testicle, but I am pretty sure mine is in the New Testicle." Daddy Mac winked at me and chuckled like we were sharing a private joke, but the laughter throughout the barn told us that a lot more than just us found it humorous. I kept waiting for Daddy Mac to speak up and correct Queenie, but he never did.

Once all the rafters were completely filled with tobacco, the barn would be heated to cure the tobacco. The fire had to burn non-stop for about a week, so a crew had to take turns manning the barn to make sure it did not burn down. Daddy Mac and my daddy usually took turns with Colin or on of the other "hands", staying up all night to stoke the fire and maintain it. In later years, kerosene heaters were used, but someone still had to be there.

One night, Shine and I wanted to stay up and help keep watch. Neither of our daddies wanted to fool with us, but Daddy Mac said we could keep him company. He warned us that there was no bathroom out there. He said he wasn't going to take a crybaby home, so we had better know what we were getting into. He said to bring a roll of toilet paper, marshmallows, hotdogs, and a coat hanger, and warm blankets. Wouldn't you know, we picked the chilliest night of the fall to camp out with him! We built a campfire and strung weenies on coat hangers and roasted them until they smelled so good, you had to eat them. When we had our fill of hot dogs, we roasted the marshmallows. Shine and I both like them gooey on the inside and practically burnt on the outside. We made enough for Daddy Mac, too. We sang a few songs like "Cum by Ya", "She'll Be Coming Around the Mountains", and "Ninety-Nine Bottles of Beer on the Wall," a most eclectic selection of songs. Every time Daddy Mac poked his head out of the barn to check on us, his eyes danced with delight that we were having such a great time.

Eventually the fire was burning down to faint embers, the time was late, and we were sleepy. The magical scent of roasted tobacco as it cured had a hypnotic effect on us. Even the hoot owls and cicadas had quieted down for the night, but not the mosquitoes! Shine and I decided the cab of Daddy Mac's truck would be a great refuge from the mosquitoes and cold. It was parked away from the barn under some trees at the edge of the field, so we grabbed our blankets and climbed in. I balled up my blanket and put half of it on the arm of the door for a cushion with the rest around me; and Shine used my thighs as her pillow, curled up on the other end of the seat with her ragged blanket. We fell sound asleep. I guess we had been asleep for several hours when we got the grits scared out of us. I felt Shine shaking my leg and couldn't see her face but could see her whites of her wide eyes in the darkness.

"Lee! Lee!" Shine was whispering, "Did you lock them truck doors?"

"No, why?" I asked, half awake.

"Shhh! Look, but don't move!" she said, slowly as she stared out of the window.

"What is that?" I whispered, looking out the window at a glint of light bobbing up and down.

It was slowly moving toward us, about waist high, up and down, up and down, shining in the moonlight.

"Look like somebody with a knife!" Shine whispered.

We both started yelling at the same time! "Mr. Alvie! Mr. Alvie!"

"Help! Daddy Mac!" I jerked Shine closer to me.

Daddy Mac came running.

As he reached the cab of the truck he yelled out, "Are ya'll all right?"

We were so scared that we could not talk, but only pointed at the glimmer in the moonlight bobbing up and down like someone with a knife walking on the other side of the truck. Daddy Mac just laughed, much to our surprise. We still did not dare move, wide-eyed.

"What's he doing?" I whispered to Shine.

Gittin' his gun, I reckon," Shine whispered back.

After a minute or two, Daddy Mac reappeared at the car window with a Mason jar with several fireflies in it! We couldn't believe we had been duped by fireflies.

"You girls are more jumpy than Freckles."

Honestly, I was fine until that reminded me: rattle snakes were out there.

CHAPTER TWELVE

~Shine~ 1966-67

When the night has come, and the land is dark
and the moon is the only light we see,
No, I won't be afraid; no, I won't be afraid,
Just as long as you stand,
Stand by me.

Ben E. King

One day when we was finished suckering tobacco, I decided I'd had enough. That was it. I had had my fill. Suckering was one of the worst jobs on the farm and you had to do it on the hottest days of the year, seemed like. Suckering is when you have to strip each tobacco plant of its tiny leaves at the bottom of the plant so that the leaves on the top will grow bigger. You do this a couple of times after you have topped off the buds of each stalk to keep them from flowering so your tobacco will fill our nicely. A lot of work goes into growing tobacco. The reason I hated suckering is you can't stand up to do it. You have to bend over to pluck them suckers off; and while you pluck the leaves, you get this sticky sap all over you. You aren't only expected to get the little suckers off, you are expected to get the dog gone nasty horn worms off, too. They be these big, huge, ugly green caterpillars with little white lines down their sides and a big horn sticking out of its head. Biggest worm you've ever seen! Mr. Alvie say you have to get ever last one of them out the field or they will destroy the whole crop. I hated those worms. I'd almost pay somebody to walk ahead of me to pop off the worms and let me do the suckering. Some people toted sudsy water to drown those boogers in and others just popped their heads off, but either way, you had to get them out of that field in case they had eggs on them.

Well, that day, I had to handle the worms and the suckering, and I decided there had to be a better way to make a living. The whole day I was in the field, my eyes burned. I wasn't sure if it was the salt from my sweat or from my tears from exhaustion and frustration, but I knew I was done. I knew it was the last time I would ever be in the field. I had my transistor radio with me in the field and made it through the hot day listening to my music. It was around 1966 so the music was real good. I would have been suckering tobacco, sweat poring off me, my little transistor radio at the end of the row where it was propped up in the sand, and me singing the TOP 100s to a rhythm as I snatched off those little suckers and those nasty worms. I mostly listened to black artists, but white folk liked them, too. I liked Junior Walker with *How Sweet It Is*, the Four Tops with *Reach Out and I'll Be There*, Tina Turner with *River Deep Mountain High*, and Percy Sledge with *When a Man Loves a Woman*. That one always tore me up. And then there was those funny ones the white people would come up with that you just had to listen to like Nancy Sinatra's *These Boots are Made for Walking*. Lee liked singing that with me when she got new boots. And Woody Guthrie's' son Arlo had his own social justice song that year called *Alice's Restaurant* that ever one went around singing if they was against the war, which was daggum near 'bout ever body. Lee said don't sing it in front of her daddy or on the farm, but we sho' sang it in the woods, almost like a prayer. Boys just a few years older than us were going off to Nam and coming home in a body bag. It was getting closer to home than we knew.

The whole afternoon I daydreamed about what I could do. I could move up North and go to school and become a secretary or a teacher. If I stayed round home, maybe I could get Mr. Alvie or somebody to loan me some money for a restaurant.

I daydreamed about serving up some of my mama's recipes because I knew people would pay for them. All afternoon I tried to get my mind off my misery, just daydreaming, I dreamed about what my menu would look like with some of my mama's special dishes and her pies and cakes. Peach pie, pecan pie, lemon meringue pie, coconut cake, caramel cake, lemon pound cake, carrot cake, and sour cream pound cake, oh she was a grand cook! She could cook all of that and more. Both of my grandmothers were good cook, too, and they all taught me how. Neither one had husbands but had lots of children, so they cooked a lot. My mother's mom thought my great granddaddy just ran off and left her to raise five children by herself and the whole time she cooked, she talked about how hard on her and how terrible it was. My father's mom did the same thing, only that grandfather died and left her, although he did die relatively young. I guess when I listened to enough of it, I decided I was better off not getting married. Now that was something to think about, too, if I was going to move up North. Men here in the fields sho' didn't have nothing to offer me, but on the other hand, I wasn't so sho' they did up North either. Lee was lucky to have Mr. Alvie. He was the kind of grandfather I would've liked to have had.

I had gone 'round to the back of Mr. Alvie's house to use his hand pump to try to get some of that dadburn resin off my hands before going on home. I had that sticky stuff all in my hair, my apron, all up and down my legs, and my hands was pure black from being covered in it.

"You can get anything you want at Adeline's Restaurant. Walk right in, don't be alarmed, Jes' a half mile from Lyndale Farms, you can get anything you want at Adeline's Restaurant.
I can bake peach pie, cream pie, pecan pie, and chocolate pie. I can bake caramel cake, coconut cake, and lemon pound cake all in the flash of an eye. Yeah! You can get anything you want at Adeline's Restaurant."

About that time, I heared a wailing in the distance. I knowed my singing was bad, but not that bad. I pumped me a drink of water, wiped my hands off on a clean part of my apron, and ran to Mr. Alvie's front yard to look down the road. It looked like Lee! She was definitely crying like she found me dead or something. I ran down the road to meet her to see what happened.

"Why are you so upset, shug?"

She could barely choke out an answer between sobs as tears skipped down her red cheeks.

Between every three words was a sob and a hiccup. "My daddy gave me a whipping with his leather belt and wouldn't stop. Look!"

I looked down at the back of her legs and that girl not only had welts up and down both legs, but blisters were starting to form.

"My Lawd, gal, what did you do?"

I put my arm around her and hugged her and tried to calm her down, but she only cried harder for some reason.

"Nothing to deserve this. Nothing that Pam and Trey weren't doing, but I was the one that got blamed for it. And my mama just stands back and lets him half beat me to death. What's wrong with him? And what's wrong with her? I don't mind getting a spanking; but I am a little too old for one, and this was a beating, not a spanking," she continued to sob.

"I don't care what you did, ain't no child deserve to be hit up like this," I said, as I spotted finger marks and fresh bruises on her arms and a bag in her hands. "You have clothes in that bag and you going to Mr. Alvie's and Miss Eltie's?"

"Yes, and I am never going home again, Shine. Ever!"

"I know how you feel, shug. I want to leave home, too. My daddy be mean to me, too. But he don't beat me like that. Dear Lord! Dear Jesus! I am going to pray your daddy gets rid of that temper of his. It don't do no body no good. Mr. Alvie has had to call him off a few people on the farm more than once."

I just kept talking patting her back as we walked back to the farmhouse. When we got to the porch, Miss Eltie was sitting on her rocker and waiting for us.

"What you girls up to? Lee what are you so upset about? Oh my, what on earth..." Miss Eltie's voice trailed off as she turned Lee around and looked over Lee's blisters and bruises.

"Vern did that, Miss Eltie."

"What on earth did you do to get that kind of spanking?"

"Miss Eltie, does it matter? She could have spilt something, mouthed off at somebody, forgot to do something, refused to do something. But should she have gotten beat up for it like a slave with a leather belt. Her legs are plum raw and now blistering."

All I could think about as I said this is slaves. Slaves, my ancestors, got it this bad and worse and they had to suck it up. No grandparents or anyone to run to. They didn't deserve it either. I guess that's why I spoke up. Just makes me sick that one human can treat another like that.

"You girls just sit here a minute and let me get you something to drink. Sweet tea, ok?" Miss Eltie left the porch as we answered her.

"Yes, Ma'am," we both said and then sat there in silence.

In a minute or two we could hear Miss Eltie on the phone just a-blessing somebody out. I couldn't make out what was being said, but I could tell she was mad. I figured it might be a while 'fore that tea was coming out; so, I hopped down off the porch column I was sitting on and started playing Doo Loo in the sand. After a while, I carried on a one-sided conversation with Lee while she rocked in Miss Eltie's chair.

"This is why I believe all us black people should get something like a payout, what they call reparations for slavery. What ya'll put us through. We ain't ever gonna get over it and you ain't ever gonna get over this. See how it feels? Just a taste, you know, but just the same, somebody should have to pay reparations. Vern gonna have to pay his reparations for this, you'll see. Miss Eltie will sho' make sure of that. You know, I worked my last day in the hot field today. I'm not going to stay around here and put up with these men. I made up my mind today I'm getting my brother to take me back to Jersey with him, and starting me a new life," I ranted.

Lee had stopped crying and just glared at me with a puzzled look. I won't sure whether she be mad at me 'cause I was leaving or because she just don't know what reparations meant. I looked back at the ground and started DooLooing again and sang. Then, I don't know what came over me. I started singing right quiet like. I sang "Peace in the Valley:

I am tired and weary, but I must toil on
Till the Lord come to call me away.
Where the morning is bright, and the Lamb is light
And the night is as fair as the day.

There'll be peace in the valley for me some day;
There'll be peace in the valley for me.
I pray no more sorrow and sadness or trouble will be,
There will be peace in the valley for me.

There flowers will be blooming, the grass will be green
And the sky will be clear and serene.
The sun ever shines giving one endless beam
And the clouds there will never be seen.
No Headaches or heartaches or misunderstands,
No confusion or trouble will be.
No frowns to defile, just a big endless smile,
There'll be peace and contentment for me.

There'll be peace in the valley for me some day;
There'll be peace in the valley for me.
I pray no more sorrow and sadness, or trouble will be,
There will be peace in the valley for me.

Then I went back to Doo Looing and pretty soon, Miss Eltie
came out before long with a tray of her homemade biscuits,
honey, and butter, and, of course, the sweet iced tea.

"Shine, what are you doing drawing in the dirt? You're
about too big for that, aren't you?"

"No'om when you miss all your childhood working in the
fields you get snatches of it back when you can, the way I
sees it."

Lee giggled. I don't know why. That was not meant to be
funny, but I was glad she was laughing.

"Mama Mac, your iced tea and your biscuits are the
absolute best. Thank you."

Lee was still hiccupping from crying as she talked. She
must have cried for a long time!

"Alvie robbed those bees this morning so that's fresh
honey, and I churned that butter myself," Mama Mac said
proudly, wiping her hands on her apron.

"Now that's what I am talking about. I was really hungry
after all that suckering today, Miss Eltie," I said, already
handing her back my glass for a refill.

We had barely finished our snack when Mr. Alvie came rushing in, not his usual calm, slow self, and I knew it was time for me to leave. Lee almost threw her plate down and wrapped her arms around her Daddy Mac's legs, and the crying started all over again. I slipped away and walked on home as he hugged and comforted her. Lee and I didn't really talk about what happened again before I left, but I saw her at the farm for the next few weeks. Mr. Alvie told me Lee could stay there as long as she wanted and that he put the fear of God in Vern that he better not ever see his grandchilren treated like that ever again.

Lee and I needed to not just leave home but leave Bishopville. Only problem was, I was old enough, and she wasn't. At least she had Mr. Alvie for a grand daddy. I ain't never had one. One died before I was born and the other one on my mother's side, ran off and left my grandma with five babies to raise by herself, and none of them ever got over that. No, I ain't ever had a grand daddy like Mr. Alvie. He'll stand by Lee.

CHAPTER THIRTEEN

~Lee~10-11 yrs. Old/5th ‑6th grade/1966-68

"Beyond the clouds, behind the rain, there are a thousand rainbows."

Unknown

I don't remember much about the time between the start of the 5th grade in the fall of 1966 to the end of the 6th grade in the spring of 1968. I do remember a tremendous pride for our soldiers in early 1966 with everyone singing patriotic songs like the *Ballad of the Green Beret*. My brother would eagerly wait for me to pick out the tune by ear at the piano so he could sing it with us (not something he did often):

Fighting soldiers from the sky
Fearless men who jump and die
Men who mean just what they say
The brave men of the Green Beret

Silver wings upon their chest
These are men, America's best
One hundred men will test today
But only three win the Green Beret.

Trained to live off nature's land
Trained in combat, hand-to-hand
Men who fight by night and day
Courage peak from the Green Berets.

Silver wings upon their chest
These are men, America's best
One hundred men will test today
But only three win the Green Beret.

Back at home a young wife waits
Her Green Beret has met his fate
He has died for those oppressed
Leaving her his last request

Put silver wings on my son's chest
Make him one of America's best
He'll be a man they'll test one day
Have him win the Green Beret.

The song made it to number one, which was amazing
considering that 1966 is considered the peak of rock and roll.
This is only a partial list of hits that year but look how many
of these we still hear: *California Dreamin'* (The Mamas and
the Papas), *When a Man Loves a Woman* (Percy Sledge),
Reach Out, I'll Be There (Four Tops), *Ain't too Proud to Beg*
(Temptations), *You Keep Me Hangin' On* (Supremes), *Wild
Thing* (Troggs*), I'm a Believer* (Monkees), *Hold On, I'm A
'Comin'* (Sam & Davis), *Good Lovin'* (Young Rascals),

River Deep, Mountain High (Ike &Tina Turner), *Mustang Sally* (Wilson Pickett), *Eleanor Rigby* (Beatles), *Try a Little Tenderness* (Otis Redding), *Summer in the City* (Lovin' Spoonful), *Got to Get you Into my Life* (Beatles), *What Becomes of the Broken Hearted* (Jimmy Ruffin), *This Old Heart of Mine* (Isley Brothers), *Monday, Monday* (Mamas and the Papas), and *Working My Way Back to You* (Four Seasons), *Good Vibrations* (The Beach Boys), *A Groovy Kind of Love* (The Mindbenders), *The Devil with the Blue Dress On/ Good Golly Miss Molly* (Mitch Ryder and the Detroit Wheels, and of course, *These Boots are Made for Walking* (Nancy Sinatra).

One reason I am taking the time to list some of these top songs is because in reviewing them, you see the change that is starting to take place in society. Adeline (Shine) and I both liked those songs. White people fell in love with Rhythm and Blues and Black people fell in love with Rock and Roll produced by white people. We were connecting more and more in music. Shine and I always had.

I don't remember little details, but I do remember the music. Perhaps I only remember it because we are still singing most of it! Other things I remember seemed so dramatic: parades and homecomings for boys from our community on leave from Viet Nam, my dad taking his anger out on me so frequently that other adults would step in, going to school in a church because our new private school had not been built, and, worst of all, Shine moving up North. I remember feeling a lot of anger because there was a lot to be angry about! I was angry that my dad was angry and took it out on me. I was upset that we were being ripped out of perfectly good, accredited schools and would most likely miss out on scholarships and opportunities because our community was fighting integration so hard. I was angry because Shine was angry at white people and at her lack of opportunity in the South. I was upset that the more than half the country was angry about the Viet Nam war and disrespectful of our soldiers. I was angry, Shine was angry, my mother was angry...all I remember is everybody being at odds with each other.

Bad things were happening all over the place. If you turned on tv at the end of 1966, you saw war demonstrations and race riots in major cities almost daily. Martin Luther King was even stoned during a March in Chicago. In January of 1967, Apollo I blew up on a launch pad killing Ed White, Gus Grissom, and Roger Chaffee. We had just visited Cape Canaveral and met them. Our neighbor, Randy Davis, at 19 years old got drafted, finished basic training and was shipped off to Viet Nam. In February 1967, before we heard from him, we kept hearing on the news how the war was escalating. Thirteen helicopters in one day had been shot down in Viet Nam at the peak of it, and then we finally started hearing from Randy. He wrote letters to everyone in the entire community. To top it all off, Elvis Pressley got married that summer, breaking the hearts of millions of us young girls.

In June and July of 1967, the race riots across the country were at an all-time high. Then in October 1967, tens of thousands of war protestors marched on Washington, and some gathered at the Pentagon. When you opened a newspaper, you either saw where the next major city had a race riot with black people demanding rights or where the next anti-war protest with mostly white people was held demanding we get out of Viet Nam. Everyone was fed up. The following year didn't get much better.

January 1968 started out with the Tet Offensive in Viet Nam. In a nutshell, the North Vietnamese broke their promise of a truce during the Tet Vietnamese holiday and waged a series of surprise attacks on US troops and the South Viet Cong while they were off for the celebration. Randy fought during Tet and received several top honors. In one of his letters home, Randy said he went to Viet Nam so some other young man less brave and not as good with a gun wouldn't have to do it. He was a marksman, and it was a good thing. It was one of the bloodiest battles of the war with tremendous losses to both sides and to civilians and was a turning point in the war. While we won the military campaign, North Viet Nam won psychologically and proved to be more fierce than we thought. The campaign left people disgusted with war.

By April 1968 when racial tensions were at an all-time high, Dr. Martin Luther King was assassinated. By that fall, Senator Robert Kennedy, President Kennedy's brother was also assassinated. I remember feeling like the world was spinning out of control and I simply wanted to have a normal childhood. I wanted so badly to talk to Shine, but my Sunshine was gone.

So, this is the vibe, the atmosphere during1966-1968 when farming was not very profitable and when my parents were incredibly hard on me. I am not saying that the atmosphere of the times is why they treated me like they did, but no one seemed to get along anywhere you looked. They certainly did seem to take their frustrations out on me, and it did not go unnoticed. Shine was constantly asking if I was ok, as well as aunts and uncles. My aunt Nancy had even had me spend a whole summer with her; and Pat Clyburn, the beauty queen who mom chaperoned, and her mom were constantly taking me home with them. For a couple of months before Shine left, I moved in with my grandparents. I had lost all hope life would get much better, and so had Shine.

Shine told me she thought the answer was we had to be well-educated so that we could find a good job and not have to depend on anyone. She told me to study hard and she was going to do her best to get educated up North. We made a pact to each be at the top of our classes.

One of the most eye-opening, insightful experiences with my mom occurred during this time. Although I knew my dad and I did not see eye to eye on a wide range of subjects, I thought my mother and I did. One day she asked me to complete a survey for Ladies Home Journal with her. She was to fill out her answers independently of me, and then we were to compare notes, discuss the differences, and send them in. The questionnaire was sent to all the 1960 Mrs. America contestants to fill out with their eldest daughter. (My mother was the SC delegate and was in the 15 finalists in 1961.) I am not exactly sure what year this happened, but I know that it was after NOW, the National Organization for Women was founded in 1966. The organization was founded to promote equal rights for women. The article was sponsored by NOW and focused on how young women of the 1960s were starting to think and feel much differently than their mothers from a generation earlier.

Now keep in mind, on the farm we could do most everything the boys could do, from driving a tractor, to baling hay, to slopping hogs. I honestly don't remember my daddy telling me I couldn't do anything on the farm. When I took Safety in 4-H, I had to learn things like changing oil in a car and changing tires. When my sister took Electricity, we learned how to wire a lamp and other things that had traditionally been chores for boys.

To give you a taste of what the atmosphere was like for Shine and me, let me give you a perspective on the timeline of things we now take for granted. Did you know that until after the Civil Right Act of 1964, women could be legally turned down for a job just because they were female or of a different race than white? In 1963-4, women made 59 cents for every dollar a man made and were kept out of the lucrative jobs. Until after the Equal Credit Opportunity Act of 1974, women could not open a bank account, have credit cards, or a mortgage in their names. As late as 1971, despite having gone through years of law school and passing every test, women could still be denied the right to plead a client's case in the court room. Mississippi was the last state to legalize allowing women to sit in a jury in 1968! As late as

1980, veterinarian colleges were still limiting how many female students could attend, no matter how good your grades were. West Point didn't admit women until 1976. No wonder my father cried when I went to Clemson, a former military college, in 1974. I could not have gone to Harvard— they didn't allow women in until the year I graduated in 1977. A woman could not take maternity leave until that year either.

Birth control pills came out in the 60s and several states banned them. If a woman lived where you could get them, she had to have her husband's signature before the doctor would prescribe them to her. All I can say is women, you have come a long way, baby!

I was completely unaware that women were held back, regarded any less than men, or limited in any way despite all of those facts until I graduated from college. So, it was in this atmosphere that my mother and I were filling out the mother/daughter questionnaire for Ladies Home Journal. She was shocked to learn that unlike her, I felt 1) it was ok for women to be lawyers and that I wanted to be one, 2) women should be able to fight in the military, 3) women should not have to ask their husbands for credit cards or money, and 4) that I felt strongly the man did not have to be the breadwinner. There were others but those stood out the most.

Just in the five short years from 1963 to 1968, my mother and I (as well as the rest of the nation) had witnessed so much change in not just thinking, but also in fashion and hairstyles. Women in the early 60s wore beehive, beauty parlor hairdos while wearing knee-length skirts and collared blouses while men still wore black and white suits. Just a few years later in the late 60s, women were sporting loose, long hair parted in the middle and wearing jeans and colorful mini-skirts while men were finally wearing colors and more casual dress. The cultural revolution was not just a mental, sexual, or transcendent thing. We could literally see it and feel it.

I am grateful that my parents helped me not feel inferior to men or feel that this revolution was wrong or that I should not evolve in it. I also believe Adeline's (Shine's) family helped her not feel inferior to other races and allowed her to grow. Although male chauvinism was prevalent in the South in the 60s, I never felt that from my father; nor did I feel there was anything I could not do. Adeline had a similar self-esteem that would serve her well.

CHAPTER 14

~Adeline~1967

*"You must hold your head high and keep those fists down.
No matter what anyone else says to you, don't let 'em get
your goat. Try fightin' with your head for a change."*

Atticus Finch in To Kill a Mockingbird by *Harper Lee*

I was so tired of working the fields. I knowed my life was meant for mo' than jes cotton fields and tobacco fields from sunup to sundown. I had done decided I was saving my money to move up North with my brothers to go to school and make something of myself. Won't nothing down here for me, as far as I could see. If I could get away from the farm and go to school, I might be able to finish and get me a real job, maybe as a secretary or a teacher. I kept thinking I would love to work with children. Anything had to be better than working out in the hot sun day after day and coming home to an ol' grumpy daddy.

Now don't get me wrong, we had our fun ever now and then in between the hard work; but it just won't much time for it when you so dog tired. One of my favorite past times was to go dancing at the club with my cousin Sally; but Daddy was so strict with his curfew, we won't able to stay out too late. One night around 1967 we went when the riots was going on all over the country and got the blackness scared right off us. Me and my cousin Sally and a couple of other girls and Bobby Butler went clubbing. It was a Sat-day night, and we was all dressed out, packed in a car, gwine uptown. We was on our way to a platter party. This night club had a DJ spinning the latest hits and we be all excited to be going up there. We won't speeding or nothing, but sure 'nough, this police car noticed us. I guess cuz we was singing and having a good old time, so he pulled us over. That cop ordered Bobby out the car and hit Bobby upside the head with a billy stick a couple of times, right in front of us girls. He said, "Nigger, where you think you going with them four pretty black girls?"

Bobby answered him politely, considering he just had the daylights knocked outs him, "We gwine up to the R & B Night Club to the Platter Party, sir."

"Well, where you been? That's a ways from heeuh!"

"We all lives out in the country, sir," Bobby said shaking and shielding his head.

Whack! The cop knocked him again with the billy stick.

"Tell me the truth, boy!" the cop bullied.

"Sir, I is telling you the truth, so help me God," Bobby pleaded, blood dripping from his temples.

Whack! The cop hit Bobby a third time, this time harder; and the girls all cringed as it cracked and let out muffled cries, not knowing what to do.

"You mighty ugly to be lucky enough to be with four pretty girls...you must be up to something," the cop said as he spit on the ground.

"No sir, these girls just my friends and I just be giving them a ride to the club, that's all. These girls are real nice Christian girls, sir. We ain't trying to cause no body no harm."

"Ain't you gonna ask what you did to get pulled over, darkie?"

"I reckon you about to tell me, sir," Bobby said hesitantly. Whack! We thought that cop done kilt him with that blow. Down he went to the ground.

The cop bent over Bobby and got nose to nose with him, saying, "I stopped you because it ain't right for you to be with four women as ugly as you is and I whacked you cuz you exist. Have a good night."

He drove off and we cleaned Bobby up and got him back into the car. We was all shaken. We couldn't report it. Heck, who you gonna report it to? The law? He was the law. We went on the platter party, but we was so mad. We was all taught from the time we could drive how to act if a cop stopped you because they don't treat you the same if you black. That told us right there what our daddies say was right. We got to be extra careful. Be polite. No sudden moves. Do what they say. Don't talk back. Don't run, Lord no, don't run. They gwine beat you up anyway.

Not too long after that, I was uptown with Sally. She'd had enough of this prejudice bull. She walked in a place that served lunch and I pointed out that the lunch counter said it served whites only. It didn't even say, "colored seated in the rear". She said, "Well, I am eating here, watch me. My grandfather was white, but my mama was black, and the white part of me is hungry."

They served her. Times was a-starting to change, but slowly.

'Bout this time I had been praying hard about whether to leave the South and go to school up North to New Jersey to be with my family up there. I wanted to get my education and seems like you can't do that when you 'spected to work on the farm all the blessed time. My hold up was that there was so much unrest and marches all over the country. The marches were not just anti-war demonstrations but racial protests as well. In July 1967 alone, there were riots in Newark, Illinois, Durham, Memphis, Detroit, Cambridge, and Milwaukee. In October, tens of thousands of war protesters marched on Washington to protest the Viet Nam War. If they won't protesting the war, they was protesting how us blacks was being treated. I just couldn't decide.

The first Sat'day in August was always like a Black celebration, like a Harvest party on the farm where all the families come together to celebrate beginning of the season. We have us a big chicken supper at the tobacco barn with a washpot full of chicken bog, a crate full of drinks and everyone brings baked cakes. That year was a going away party of sorts for me because I finally decided and announced it gonna be my last. Lee said tobacco season gwine take twice as long cuz nobody else could string as fast as me. I don't know if that be the truth, but Lee sho' would slow it down! Ha! Anyways, I knowed I was going to miss my friends in South Carolina, but I knowed I had to get my schooling in if I want to get anywhere in life, too. Seem like all the boys I knew been hauled off to Viet Nam, so not much good prospects for a husband left 'round here. If anything was to be, looked likes it was gonna be left up to me. Daddy agreed and seemed to act indifferent when Peggy and I made plans to move up North with my middle brother. He lived in New Jersey, and I could go to school there.

My brother, Jacob, came and got us, and I enrolled in Hatch Junior High that fall. I did all right not to have any more education in the South than I did, but I did have some catching up to do. I liked school. I made up my mind I was not going to stop learning. I was expected to work, too, and that was alright because you didn't have to work in the fields in the hot sun up North. You could waitress or be a clerk in a store or something like that.

I knew my ticket out of the fields was getting a good education. I went to the school in the morning and worked at night because my brother expected me to pay for my room and board. The first day I introduced myself at school, I said, "My name is Shine and I jes moved here from South Carolina." The whole room started snickering, gradually turning into such loud laughter that the teacher had to shush them. I just hung my head. I thought it was my Southern accent, and maybe it was a little of that. But, thankfully, a sweet little girl that became my friend who sat behind me came up to me during recess to tell me what the laughter was all about.

She said, "Sweetheart, what's your real name? I can't be...what you said."

"No, it isn't," I told her. "My daddy named me 'Adeline' at birth, but my mama always called me 'Sunshine' because of a song she sung me, 'You are My Sunshine'. It got shortened to just plain 'Shine' over the years. Why is that so funny to you all?"

"Well, it wasn't really funny. Around here no Afro-American person would never let anyone call them 'Shine,' don't you know that?"

"No! I didn't. I've been called that all my life."

"Did some white person name you that? I can't imagine a black person calling you that," she said, looking truly surprised.

"Why?" I asked.

"Because the term 'shine' is a derogatory term for black people here. So many black boys shine shoes on the streets and in the airports, I think that's where it came from. They will say things like, 'He is just a shine looking for a nickel.' Your mama wouldn't have called you that. Sunshine maybe, but not plain Shine. Who named you that?"

"Now that I think about it, my white playmate on the farm, Lee...I think she was the one that called me that first, and it just stuck." Then it was me looking surprised. How could Lee do that to me? Surely, she knew. She was educated.

"All right, from now on I am 'Adeline,'" I said.

I certainly would have a talk with Miss Lee when I got back home!

"What is your name, dear heart?" I asked hoping to make a friend.

"Mary. I need to introduce you to my cousin Rose. She moved here from the South, too. Her parents sent her up here to have her baby."

"I hear there is a lot of that going on."

Mary sighed. "Well, in Rose's case, she was ambushed by several white men. By the time she realized she was pregnant, her mother convinced her it would be easier for her to move up here and have the baby rather than to stay in South Carolina and try to convict white people for their crime."

"Is she going to keep the baby?" I asked.

"I think so. It would definitely be easier to raise to raise a half-white baby here."

"Or half-black," I joked.

"You know if she had been a white girl and that had been black men, they would've been convicted and would be lucky to not get lynched before they made it to court," Mary said.

"I know that's the truth," I said. "I heard tell of so many black girls being raped in the South and none of them ever turned those guys in. Not one! I know some of them moved north to have those babies and some gave them up for adoption and some kept them. So many stories I can't even talk about."

Mary and I shared many stories and secrets from then on. She helped me understand the culture up North and I introduced her to Southern cooking. (She loved my collards and cornbread but did not like grits or fatback too much.) I helped her understand Southern dialects and she introduced me to young men at her church. I fell in love with one of the young men. He was tall and funny and smart. And boy, could he dance! He taught me to not only do the Twist and the Jerk, but also the Harlem Shuffle and the Mashed Potato. He would sing Marvin Gaye songs and other Motown songs to me and make all the other girls jealous. We had such a good time together. He had relatives near mine in South Carolina and we talked about someday moving down together. Less than a year after we started dating, he got drafted and sent to Viet Nam. He wrote me almost every week. I was so in love!

Colored Seated in the Rear

CHAPTER FIFTEEN

~Lee~11 yrs old /6th grade/ fall of 1967

*"A life spent making mistakes is not only more honorable,
but more useful than a life spent doing nothing."*

George Bernard Shaw

My mother started teaching kindergarten at the Academy rather than out of our house in exchange for some of the tuition for the three of us. Over the years, she also owned a beauty shop called the Silhouette Salon, a floral shop called the Little Florist, and co-owned a wig shop that carried Holiday Magic Make-up (led by a wonderful man named Ben Gay III who, interestingly and unknowingly, later became a friend and mentor to me)—all while teaching. She made sure we were equally busy with our time, shuttling Trey, Pam, and me from 4-H club meetings, to scout meetings to music and dance lessons, art lessons and baton twirling lessons. I wasn't that great at any of those activities, but it was a great diversion from the awful news on tv about the war and from the news that Shine was going to live up North.

Of all the activities Mama had us involved in, I probably excelled most in 4-H. From the first gold star for demonstrating how to change a baby's diaper to the first blue ribbon for canning something at the fair, I liked winning and achieving with 4-H. Shine would help me think of demonstrations and let me practice on her, even though she didn't come to our meetings. In fact, no black children came to them. She could cook and sew and would have loved 4-H. When I was doing a demo for a peach milkshake and the shake tasted like everybody else's, Shine told me to mix eggs and milk and a little sugar on the stove first and then put it in the blender with ice and frozen peaches. It made all the difference and I won. Then when I entered a corn muffin contest, Shine told me to use a pinch of salt and pinch of sugar and a tablespoon of my grandaddy's honey—and it won, too—for county and state!

When I was in the sixth grade in 1967, I did a project that involved interviewing several neighbors about what their families ate for breakfast, lunch and dinner. Since I lived on the farm, our neighbors included poor tenant farm families on our road, too. This one particular couple that I will call Jeb and Essie, had five children and did not have a garden or hogs or chickens like most farm families. Essie had one eye that went one way and one that went the other, and her jaw was always slap full of snuff. Jeb just seemed downright lazy and didn't work half the time. Essie agreed to let me interview her for my project. I was shocked when I went in their house. Unlike Lizzie's neat home with furniture, theirs had none, except for a table, two chairs and a filthy mattress on the floor. You could see the ground underneath the house through the cracks in the planks. The whole house was not much bigger than my bedroom.

"Have a seat, Miss Lee, and let's me see if I can help you, uh huh," Essie smiled with her snaggled-tooth grin while I tried to follow her eyes.

"Right here?" I asked, not sure which chair her eyes were focused on.

"Yessum. What do you need to know, um hum?" Essie was putting cornrows in her hair while she talked to me, but instead of the braids being neat and flat against her head like most of the black women I knew, they were going all over the place and sticking out every which away. Her hair sort of fit her personality. Her jaw jutted out with a thick pouch of tobacco, and she spit tobacco juice as she talked.

"Well, I am going to ask you about your family's nutrition," I said as I opened my notebook.

"New Trition?" she questioned me, cocking her head as one eye shot straight up and one looked me dead on. "I don't think we got's anything new at all. It all be old. What you talking 'bout, Miss Lee?"

As I stifled a laugh, I said, "You know, Essie, nutrition, what you eat. I am going to ask you what you have for breakfast, lunch, and dinner every day for several weeks, ok?"

"Ok, I got it, um hum, I gots it." Essie grinned, sitting back in her chair, then spitting.

"Alright, tell me what you had for breakfast yesterday morning," I started.

"We had crayfish for breakfast. I fry 'em up every morning, uh hum,"

"Crayfish? You mean crawfish?"

"Same thing, um huh."

"Essie, I thought you could only get those in New Orleans. You get those from the A&P in Bishopville?" I asked, wondering how they could afford such a delicacy every morning.

"No, chile, we gets 'em right out the ditch, right out there," she exclaimed as she pointed toward the road. "You just dig 'em out the mud."

"Can you get one so I can see," I prodded, not believing crawfish were in our ditches, much less that she was eating them for breakfast.

"We ain't got no 'frigerator, so I will have to go fetch one fresh. I can cook some up for you if you is hungry, um hum. Pretty Boy, how 'bout go get some cray for Miss Lee out de ditch." Essie yelled out to her oldest son.

Pretty boy came back shortly with a hand full of white stuff wiggling in his hand.

"Let me see what you have there."

Pretty boy opened his little hands. "Oh my gosh, that's grub worms," I recoiled. "You don't eat those, do you?"

"Yeah, that be good, too, head and all." His mama confirmed. "Lemme fix some for you."

"I don't want any, thanks," I held my stomach, trying not to lose it.

"So, at lunch what did you have yesterday?" I tried to get our conversation back on track.

"I had me some more crayfish and some poke salad," Essie said, then spit.

"Poke salad?"

"Yeah, baby, don't you know what dat is?" She reached under the table and withdrew a sack of weeds that looked like spinach with red edging along the ribs of the stalks and berries that were so dark in color that Daddy Mac called them "ink berries." "Yeah, um hum. That make up a good salad and sometimes we find a quail egg or two to put in it or we scramble 'em with some grubs." Essie sat there smiling at me like that was perfectly normal.

I sat there fake-smiling back at her for a few seconds too long, trying to imagine. She also told me something me about using chicory to make a drink similar to coffee and using sassafras to make a tea at lunch. I tried to take notes to get all of it down, unfamiliar with half the things she mentioned.

"So, tell me what you had for supper last night," I asked, bracing myself, hoping it wasn't roadkill.

"Well, let's see, las' night it was 'coon. The boys went coon hunting and got some right nice sized ones. Tonight, we making a bog with squirrel with some rice Mr. Colin Reddick gave us. Just boiling 'em up together, um hmm. Add a little salt and pepper. What's wrong, Miss Lee?"

"That doesn't sound too appetizing to me!" I shuttered.

"You like chicken bog?"

"Yes, ma'am.

"Well, now, it tastes like that, just a little more flavorful, um huh." Essie smiled as her untethered eyes wiggled in different directions towards me.

Essie proceeded to tell me that they had the same things, meal after meal, every week, when I would come to interview her. Each week, I would go home and cry and ask Mama what we could do about it. Her answer was always the same: Essie and Jeb had a plot of land right there just like all the other hands to grow a garden, raise chickens and hogs and maybe even have a cow. If they were too lazy to tend to a garden and to animals, then she didn't feel too charitable. Poor Essie, how could I help her?

In the middle of my project, Daddy brought home meat processed from one of his beef cows and I helped wrap the steaks, hamburgers and roasts in freezer paper and marked it with the date. We had a huge 25-cubic ft. freezer on the back porch and about a third of it was already filled with strawberries, butterbeans, field peas, corn, squash, and okra. We had enough meat to fill the rest of the freezer! It was so full, that I knew that Mama and Daddy would not miss a few packages, so, without asking, I took several packages to Essie and her family.

I finished my 4-H nutrition project and was forever changed from it. Shine assured me her family didn't eat like that; but everyone on our road had their own weird habits, most of which were not very healthy and none of which were as pitiful as Essie and Jeb's.

One day after I finished the project, I came home from school and Daddy had a visitor. It was unusual for Daddy to be at the house in the middle of the day—he was always at the farm. I grabbed a snack and looked for my mom.

"Mama, what on earth is Daddy doing out on the back porch with the Sheriff?"

"He and Mr. Liston are installing some hidden cameras, but don't say anything to anyone about them, especially not Shine or Lizzie. I don't think they are the ones stealing the meat out of our freezer, but I don't won't them to alert the fool that did."

I almost choked on my snack.

Weeks went by and I did not dare take anything out of the freezer. Then one day I saw Shine down at the farm, and she told me Essie and Jeb's oldest boy got arrested for stealing food out of our freezer. I could not believe it.

As things escalated in the Viet Nam War with troops increasing from more than 175,000 in mid-1965 to over 410,000 by the end of 1966, peace demonstrations, marches, and race riots became common occurrences in the news. We still had three television stations and our local WAGS radio station in Bishopville with unbiased reporting like that of today. Everyone was glued to the news because of the war. We went to church every Wednesday night for Prayer meeting because we felt like the world sure needed it, went to the high school football game every Friday it was in Bishopville because those boys sure needed our support, and showed up for church every Sunday morning because our little church sure needed every member there—and Daddy Mac was still giving out silver dollars at the end of every year. Between the three stations and WAGS and church, everybody knew everything, and I do mean everything, going on in Bishopville and in the entire nation, if not the world.

And there was one other way—party lines. Back then very few phone lines were private. Usually, three or four neighbors would share a line. You would literally have to wait for one person to get off before you could take your turn. If you picked up the phone, you could hear the other party talking so nothing was private. We happened to be on the same line as my grandmother and the preacher!

I usually knew one of them were listening in because many times I could hear someone breathing besides my caller. It was not fun being a teenager and being on a party line with your grandmother and the preacher, but I am sure they were not thrilled about it either.

As soon as I got home talking to Shine at the farm, I called one of my 4-H friends to confide about the meat from the freezer and ask her advice what to do.

"Debbie, you know all that beef my daddy had butchered a month ago?"

"Yeah, we had some of it last night that my parents bought. I was sure good."

"Well, you know when I did the 4-H project I told you about the family that was eating grubs and stuff out of the ditch because they didn't have any money?"

"Yes, but don't you think that crazy Essie was pulling your...."

"No, no, they were really eating that way! She wanted to cook me up some! But listen, Debbie, I felt sorry for them; and when Daddy butchered that cow, I took some meat out of the freezer without telling my parents and took it down to Essie and Jeb," I confided.

"Well, that was really sweet of you..."

"No, you, don't understand," I continued to confess, "Daddy put up cameras and they just arrested Essie and Jeb's oldest boy for taking food out of the freezer!"

We both went silent. We both heard it. Breathing. Heavy breathing.

"Did you hear that?" Debbie asked. "Someone's on the line with us."

"Oh, great."

Sure enough, it wasn't twenty-four hours before I knew that it was my grandmother who had been listening in. And, of course, I was in big trouble, and got grounded: not for giving food away, but for not asking if I could and not interceding on the young man's behalf.

CHAPTER 16
~Adeline~1968-1969

"I thought maybe the difference between white folks and colored is just this matter of reading and writing and I made up my mind I would know my letters."

Mary McLeod Bethune

The love of my life was to come home from Viet Nam just before Christmas. We had his mama's house, our house, the whole street, decorated for him to come home and a homecoming party planned at the church. I had never been more excited. The whole town of Bishopville had a habit of doing a parade for those boys, too. He came home, all right. He came home in a body bag. It broke my heart. Just tore me all up. I still can't talk about it. My heart ain't never been the same since. That's when that war became real. I realized that not just me, but many folks, black and white, all colors, had lost thousands of boys my age all across the country. Thousands. Boys just out of high school that had not had a chance to start their lives yet were killed in a senseless war. It was just another thing the government was wasting money on that could be spent on reparations or getting rid of poverty or helping our own people have a better life.

I threw myself into my schoolwork to ease my pain. I liked school and I studied hard. Eventually I switched to working in the day and going to school at night and I got my diploma. I was a secretary for a while and a nursing assistant for a while, too. Then came my big chance. I moved to Washington, DC, and was able to get my associates degree. Life was much more fast paced in the big city than on the farm, but I got used to it. I had to take a bus everywhere, and I thought of Miss Rosa Parks often, and thanked her most every day. The signs saying "Colored Seated in the Rear" had mostly disappeared. I did not take it for granted.

While I was in Washington, Rev. Martin Luther King was assassinated. We felt like the headway black people had made was snatched from us with one bullet. I was with a bunch of girls working in an office and everything came to a halt. I, along with the whole of Washington DC, it seemed, were in shock and mourning, as if a close family member had died. I thought I would never get over it. Dr. King had peacefully brought so much attention to the inequality, the inhumanity, and the plight of the black race in America. We didn't know if things would go backwards or if anyone would lead us forward. It was an awful feeling of anxiety and longing. Going to vigils only made it worse because some fool usually decided to get violent and riot.

Then one day I got some good news that cheered me up, at least for a minute. My dream came true—I landed a job working with handicapped children at a school. My job was to make sure they got on the right bus safely and some other things like that, getting them from one classroom to another. I was so happy to see the little black children returning day after day to the same school, getting their education, not having to work like we were made to down South. I could see Dr. King's work in motion. I could see black and white kids studying together and going to recess and doing the things little children are supposed to do at that age, but I also realized how much I missed out on. It made me angry. I was angry about a lot of things besides just Dr. King getting shot. I was angry about not being educated correctly, angry about my mama dying on me and the love of my life getting killed.

I was angry about the way my daddy and Peggy treated me. I was angry about how blacks were treated. I was angry about all our boys getting killed in Nam, especially the one I thought I was going to marry. Heck, I was still angry about my great granddaddy leaving my great grandmother because that had been drilled into me. Then the little speck of hope I had came crashing down in the late 60s when Rev. King was assassinated. I was angry about that, too. At the time, I thought he was our last hope that things would ever be right between the blacks and the whites.

Another thing that I was angry about is that you couldn't trust anyone, but worst of all you couldn't trust the government. They would do things like set up a program to help you out to give you more money, then tax you to death to take it back. They would make you think you were getting ahead long enough to get your vote, then come tax season, you would realize you have done been duped. I still haven't figured out the purpose of it, unless it was to distract our attention from something else; but the government even wanted us to believe they had landed on the moon! To this day I believe they filmed it in Hollywood. You could tell all the shots on television were reenactments and were fake, but all them white people believed that we had really launched a little rocket with a space capsule on it and landed on the moon. The little crawler on the tv set even said some of that stuff was re-enacted but them white folks still believed hook, line, and sinker that that spaceship really did land on the moon. Wonder what they really did with all that money they say they spent on that little project? We sure could have used it in the black community. We could have used it for reparations.

Our society was coming a long way and so was I. The pain of the memories made it harder and harder to go back home, but I knew that one day I would retire and save enough money to move back to Bishopville. Bishopville was quieter, safer and it was home. I would buy me a little place and have me a little garden.

Of course, I got homesick occasionally, and most of my extra money I saved for getting me a bus ticket back to Bishopville. I made sho' it was round trip though. No way was I going to get stuck down South again.

I remember the first time I got a ticket home, and nobody knew I was coming. Now, you know Daddy didn't have no phone, so when I got to the bus station in Bishopville, who do you think I called? I called Mr. Alvie to come pick me up. So, here I was, a pretty little black teenager in downtown, down in segregated Bishopville on Main Street in the center of town, sitting outside with my raggedy old luggage waiting for a handsome, rich white man to pick me up. I thought I would have a little fun, so when he drove up, I made sure the prissy little white women at the counter were watching as I threw my arms around my neck and greeted him.

"Mr. Alvie! Mr. Alvie, I am so glad to see you! Oh, I have missed you so much! How is everybody?"

I wasn't lying—I really had missed everybody—even him and Miss Eltie.

"Well, hello, Shine!" Mr. Alvie turned red as he pried my arms from around him and stood back to look at me. "Gracious gal! You all growed up on us, now haven't you!"

"Mr. Alvie, I wore my prettiest dress for you to pick me up in—I made it myself!"

"My, my now, you just like your mama. That woman could sew. Can you cook, too, Shine?"

"Mr. Alvie, quit calling me Shine. That be a derogatory term up North. I ain't Shine no more!
Please put my stuff in your truck and let's go." My attitude changed in a hurry.

When we got in the car I explained to Mr. Alvie, he would have to call me by my real name, Adeline, because in the North, I got laughed at for being called Shine. Shine was a derogatory name for the poor little black boys that shined shoes and up North, they was a lot of those on the street corners, in the bus stations and airports all trying to make a dime. I was so tired of hearing about it, I just went back to plain old Adeline.

"Adeline is a beautiful name, Shine. I remember when your daddy gave you that name."
He just couldn't help his self. He say Adeline then kept calling me Shine right on.

We got out to the country, to Stokes Bridge Road, and low and behold, Mr. Alvie be pulled up in the field where they be picking cotton.

"Mr. Alvie!" I said pretty quick like. He was already getting out. "What in hell's bells you think you doing?"

"I brought you home. I thought you might...."

"Now, Mr. Alvie, I tell you right now I ain't picking no cotton. I ain't gone all the way up North to get a daggum education for you to bring me back and dump me in your cotton field. I will just tell you that right now!"

"Hey, Girl! Hey Shine! Look at you!"

"Hey Shine, oh my you is all grown up!"

"Oh, my is that Miss Ruths baby? Look what a pretty young woman she be! Come over here, Shine and hug your Aunt Betty."

"Shine, I just brought you by to see your friends," Mr. Alvie said laughing. "I know you need to get home and rest up. I 'm not going to get you to work today, but if you want to tomorrow..."

"Mr. Alvie, I know you pulling my leg. My Daddy probably got a list a mile long for me anyways. And please, call me Adeline. Show me some respect." I then explained to everybody why they ain't nobody gonna be calling me Shine no more.

I stayed awhile and visited with my people and played with Mr. Alvie's rat terriers while I watched Mr. Alvie weigh everybody's cotton. Ain't nobody even come near what I used to pick. Mr. Alvie said I held the record on Lyndale

Farms, and he was pretty sure for the county and the state. I could pick 305 lbs. of cotton in one day! No one else could come near that record, male or female. He also said I was the fastest stringer in tobacco, bar none. But they ain't no way of knowing it for sure. Mr. Alvie saying it was good enough for all of us. I was pretty darn fast.

When Mr. Alvie had his figures done, he came round the side of the truck and opened the door for me and said, "Miss Adeline, you ready to go home?"

He bowed like he was my butler or chauffeur as I got in, showing me the respect I had asked for, went around the truck tipping his hat to everyone else, and off we went. Mr. Alvie whistled "What a Friend We Have in Jesus" all the way to my house. Onliest, he didn't whistle it like normal people—he whistled it through his teeth. His special way of whistling was one of the many things that made that man so special, that and his Old Spice.

CHAPTER 17

~Lee~12-13 yrs old/7th grade/fall 1968-1969

*"Remember that not getting what you want
is sometimes a wonderful stroke of luck"*

Dalai Lama

I am not sure how Mom kept up with our schedules or when to have us at what activity. Pam, Al, and I all had different interests. If I remember correctly, I had student body rep meetings after school on Mondays, and then had horseback lessons. On Tuesdays and Thursdays, I had baton and gymnastics while Pam had tap and ballet. On Wednesdays I had art lessons while Trey and Pam had Scouts, followed by St. Matthews Methodist Church prayer meeting. On Thursday night I had ballroom dancing. On Fridays I usually had to babysit someone's kids. Saturday was chores. Church was Sunday and Sunday night was MYF. I studied extra hard in school, just as I promised Shine. And it paid off. I was the valedictorian at my 7th grade graduation.

Robert E. Lee Academy only had seven grades that year and after that, you had to go to public school until they raised enough money to build more classrooms. The students held delightful "Hootenanny" Talent shows and the parents held

145

outrageous "Womanless Weddings" to raise money for the Academy, among other things.

The tradition was to hold a seventh grade graduating ceremony. The school did not have an auditorium yet, so our ceremony was held in the church where our classes used to be when the academy first opened. The theme of the speech I was assigned to write was "standing up for what you believe in." Of course, I had no trouble voicing that. In fact, more than one of my teachers were more than a little apprehensive about what I would be saying. The real kicker was that despite standing up for what I believed in at thirteen years old, it didn't seem to matter. Two of the most important people in my life that I wanted to be in the sanctuary to hear my speech and celebrate my achievement were not allowed to be there. I told my parents that I wanted to invite Lizzy and Shine. They both looked at me like I had two horns on my head all of the sudden, expressionless. I told my teachers I wanted to invite them, and they said I could not invite "colored folks". I told the headmaster and he looked down his nose at me with his glasses sliding off, and just said, "absolutely not!" He tried to cover it by saying we didn't have much room in the sanctuary for anyone but parents, grandparents and siblings. I told him my siblings did not want to come, but that did not matter. I told him Lizzy was like my mom and Shine was like a sister. That did not matter either. He rolled his eyes. So much for standing up for your rights.

I tweaked my speech to add fervently that adults should listen to children more often when they *know* in their hearts their child is right, whether it be about racism, upholding a Christian principle or a law of the land, or an invitation to their special event. I looked our headmaster squarely in the face and watched him squirm as his face turned bright red.

After the ceremony, all of us went to the choir room to take off our graduation gowns and get our final report cards. While we were busy looking over our grades, then saying our goodbyes to each other, I noticed one of my friends having a major melt down, shaking and saying, "Daddy's g-going to k-kill me! I c-ccan't g-go home!"

Everyone else was backing away from her or leaving the room. I went over to her and put my arms around her and said, "Meghan, what's wrong?"

"I failed my grade again. My parents will k-kill me. They will beat the stuffing out of me. I'm n-not going home. Oh, my God, I c-can't go home," she sobbed.

My excitement over being valedictorian quickly faded. My heart hurt so badly for her.

"Oh, Sweetie, don't cry. You can go home with us. You don't have to go to your house," I promised.

"Oh, please see if I c-can ride home with y'all. I just can't go home; I j-just can't!" she pleaded.

I held her and let her sob until she calmed down, then assured her, "I will get my mom and dad to talk to your parents. They can keep them from beating you. I will make sure of it."

My mind was churning. I wasn't sure how in the world I was going to get one child abuser to deal with another child beater, but this ought to be interesting, I thought. As soon as Meghan composed herself, we walked back to the front of the church to find my parents. Most everyone had left by then. When we approached them, I told them that she had flunked her grade and was terrified of going home. I asked if it was ok if she went home with us for a little bit first. They agreed.

I said, "Great, because she needs y'all right now. She needs y'all to go talk to her parents for her. Could you take us home and let me stay with her while you two talk to them?"

"Sure," both said.

"Meghan, you can even spend the night with us," my mother added.

"Great. You need to tell them it is against the law to beat your kids. Can you tell them there are better ways to handle things? Meghan can't help it if she has a learning disability or whatever is holding her back in school. Learning comes easy to one kid and music comes easy to another, like it does to her. She can't be hit for things she has no power over. That's like beating me because I can't play the piano like she can. I wish I could. I could practice five times a week and I am still not going to play like her. And beating a child…when has that solved anything? Please, you tell them it DOES NOT," I said emphatically, feeling the blood rising to my cheeks.

Then I turned to Meghan and said, "Come on Meghan, let's go get in the car."

I glanced back over my shoulder and told my parents, "Y'all might want to stay in here a minute and pray about what you are going to say to them."

My parents stood in the in the empty sanctuary as we left. I don't' know what they did after Meghan and I got in the car, but they stayed in the church for a good while. We rode home in silence with Meghan still whimpering. When we got home, they left to go visit Meghan's parents and Meghan spent the night with us, despite her father calling and demanding she come home. Daddy wouldn't let her go. Lord, have mercy. God only knows the conversation those four had. I don't know what happened between Meghan and her parents when she finally went home. I do know that she went to public school the next year, and not long after that she got pregnant and moved away. I went to public school the next year too, but little did I know what was about to happen to me.

That fall just before school opened, I went with my mother to register for eighth grade at Bishopville High School. I was really excited to get to go to public school and go to bigger classes, pep rallies and to school with older teenagers. I sat outside Mr. Teal's office a really long time before my mom came back out with my test scores, notes from teachers and report cards in hand.

"Well, it's official! You are going to be skipping the 8th grade and go straight into the 9th!"

"What do you mean? Nobody asked me...I want to graduate with my own class. I don't want to move up," I protested.

"It's a real honor. I thought you would be excited," she said, pushing me toward the exit door.

"Excited? That's taking a year of your childhood away from me. What are you thinking?"

"Well, Daddy and I will have three kids in college all at the same time if we...."

"So, this is about convenience for you and Daddy? You are still going to have three children in college at the same time, even if I go a year early. What is the real reason? No one thought to ask me what I thought?"

"Well, part of it is since the academy is not accredited you won't be getting a scholarship you could have gotten and...and..." my mother started fidgeting, "we didn't think this was a decision for you."

"Unbelievable! You can't even say just once that you are proud of my grades or congratulations for being valedictorian or 'Lee, congratulations, you are so smart, you get to move up a grade,' can you?"

"You know we are proud of you!" she looked shocked.

"You never say it. You are pretty vocal about a lot of other stuff. You and dad can't wait to get me out of the house. Is that it? If you look at it from that perspective, well, guess what, I can't wait to leave!"

By the time the conversation got to this point, we had walked over from the high school to the Dairy-O next door where we had already planned to get broasted chicken to take home. I am not sure what broasted meant because I have never seen it sold anywhere else before or since. I assume it was broiled and roasted chicken, which is how I felt my feelings and nerves were at this point, so I asked Mama if I could order a large chocolate milkshake with whipped crème and a cherry on top, thinking that would help. Mama agreed, much to my surprise. She started talking with another farmer's wife who drove up while I ordered the food. I placed the order, then stood to the side waiting, dreaming about being able to come over to the Dairy-O for ice cream every day after high school. What a perk! All of the sudden, I heard a familiar voice and laugh coming from a group of people at the picnic table on the side. I cocked my head and listened. It was indeed a familiar voice. It was Shine! There was no mistaking that laugh!

"Shine, Shine! What are you doing here?" I threw my arms around her neck and almost knocked her off the picnic table. "I am so glad to see you! I thought you were in New Jersey!"

She stood up and took both my arms in her hands and disengaged them from around her neck and held them out in front of her and said, "Yes and I am back for a visit. Don't you be calling me 'Shine'. Didn't you know that is an insult to an Afro-American? You knew that when you nicknamed me that, didn't you...didn't you...you...?" She grinded her teeth.

"Shine!" I said in shock. I honestly couldn't remember what her real name was!

"You honky!" a black girl sitting with her said.

"You white..." another girl started to say.

Shine interrupted her with her hands up. "Y'all stop calling her names. This between me and her. Why did you call me 'Shine'?" she asked, pointing her finger at me.

"Well, you know why, silly. It's short for Sunshine. What's wrong with that?"

"Up North they say that is an insult to Afro-Americans and you should have known it," Shine said as she stepped toward me with her head bobbing and her hands on her hips.

I backed up a step or two.

"First of all, why 'Afro-American'? Is it not proper to say colored or black anymore? We are still white for heaven's sake. And no, Shine is my nickname for you, like Daddy Mac calls me Sweetpea. Just shortened what your mama called you and I don't know why on earth 'Shine' would be a bad thing—shine like a star..." my voice trailed off.

"I want you to call me 'Adeline' and act like you got some class. Just 'cause we raised on a farm, we don't have to act like we ain't got no class. Yes, call black people Afro-Americans, please. We are Americans, too. Not just you white people that act like you own the whole dang country."

"Well, welcome home, Adeline. I guess I was mistaken. I thought you would be glad to see me. I sure did miss you," I said, not hiding my disappointment.

"I'm sorry, shug. You kind of caught us in the middle of a political conversation. Maybe it was the timing. I missed you, too, my old friend," Adeline apologized as she hugged me.

"I am glad you are here. Mama just took me over to Bishopville High to enroll me in Eighth Grade for next year, only..."

"Eighth grade? Chile, I can't believe you old enough for the eighth grade."

"Yeah, well, the problem is my mother moved me up to the ninth without telling me and I'm pretty upset about it," I said, biting my lip."

"Girl, why you all upset about that? Dang, that's yo' ticket out. Look at you and your smart butt! Finally paid off. Good for you. I told you to study hard and get out of here, now, didn't I?"

"Yeah, but..."

"Listen, Lee, if you can get out of here sooner, just do it. Where are you going after high school? Clemson?"

"Probably. Maybe somewhere smaller. Hey, Daddy Mac is on County Council if he can help you with anything political," I said.

"No, we were talking about national stuff like the government trying to fool us into thinking they put a man on the moon this month. Did you see that? You could tell it was filmed in Hollywood. It was so fake."

"Now, Adeline," it didn't seem natural coming off my lips just yet, "Adeline, they did send those men to the moon. I did see it on television. It was real."

"Lee, you believe ever thing you see on television?" she snickered. The other girls were clapping and snickering behind her.

"No, but I have been to Cape Canaveral and the Kennedy Space Center. It is real! I saw the space suits and the rockets and the control center—everything."

"So, you family done drove all the way to Florida and went to see that? Vern must have thought something was up to go all the way down there to see for his self. See?"

"Adeline, the whole family went. You know Trey is into rockets. And we all went to the new Disney World in Florida too.

"Girl, that is nothing but the government trying to get us to believe that they are doing that. I don't know what they up to, but what pure manure," one of the girls on the picnic table said.

"That's right," Adeline said, "Ain't no little white man put a little spaceship on the end of a rocket with dynamite on it and sent it to the moon."

All three girls were doubled over laughing. I wasn't.

"Adeline don't be ridiculous. They have no reason to lie to us about that," I said.

The girls all laughed again, then she said, "Of course they do, they got to explain why they not paying us."

"Paying you for what?" I asked.

"Paying us reparations. They gonna make out like they spent it all going to the moon and that doggone war," she said, and the laughter stopped. "And now that silly white people's park built in a swamp in Florida. Lawd, ain't ya'll something?"

"You have mentioned reparations to me over the years before. Why do you think the government owes *you* reparations for slavery when you were not a slave, and your ancestors only *may* have been? Have you personally researched it? Do you know for sure? I was not your slave master; Daddy Mac was not your slave master. Why do you think *our* taxes should pay you for *anything*?"

"To right a wrong, dear heart, to right a wrong," Adeline answered.

"That isn't going to help anything. We aren't the ones that did that. You are going to hold us responsible for what our ancestors did, are you?"

"No, but we can hold the government responsible," she said.

"That's right," the other two chimed in.

"But we, you and me and our community, we *are* the government. We are not your ancestors or the people that did that. Besides, did you know that at the time of the ratification of the Constitution of the United States, there were less than 50,000 slaves in America and the vast majority were white slaves?"

"What? I've never heard of white slaves," Adeline said.

"Look it up. Indentured servants. Treated like slaves, had to work off their trip to America and many had to work it off for a generation or so. Then when cotton plantations started springing up, the slave trade switched from Europe to Africa. Black people owned slaves, too."

"No, they didn't!" one of the girls scowled.

"Oh, yes, they did. In fact, some bought and sold for a living, not just owned them for working purposes. Look it up if you don't believe me. I am sure some of my relatives were probably indentured servants from Europe, but I am grateful I am here and not there. I am grateful for what this country has to offer, and you should be, too. Would you rather be back in the slums of Africa?"

"Oh, Lee you just a child. You don't know what you are talking about. Go on with your crazy self. I sho' am glad to see you though."

And with that, Adeline gave me another hug. My mother was calling me over to the car, saying she had the milkshake and the chicken already. Sounded like the North was beginning to change Adeline. Or had she always been this way?

CHAPTER 18\
~Adeline~1969-1970

"Giving up doesn't always mean you are weak. Sometimes it means that you are strong enough to let go."

Dr. Phil

Note from Editors:
Adeline (Shine aka Sunshine) was mentally and emotionally drained at this juncture writing the book. She could not continue helping Lee remember the past. She no longer wanted to document details and Lee's trips were becoming futile. Memories were just too painful. Lee could not even get enough information from her to piece together what may have happened. Later Adeline regained her perspective and renewed her efforts. In the meantime, Lee went through their notes and let this chapter capture some of the quotations that

they both collected for the book. In many cases, they had collected the same quotes.

"Most of the shadows of this life are caused by our standing in our own sunshine."

Ralph Waldo Emerson

"Life is God's gift to us; what we do with it is our gift to God."   Unknown (and Mama Bessie)

"The smallest act of kindness is worth more than the grandest intention."   Oscar Wilde

"Courage is being scared to death and saddling up anyway."   John Wayne

"And the day came when the rush to remain tight in a bud was more painful than the rush it took to blossom."

Anais Nin

"It's not whether you get knocked down, it's whether you get up."   Vince Lombardi

"Sometimes I have believed as many as six impossible things before breakfast."

Lewis Carroll

"Logic will get you from A to B. Imagination will take you everywhere."   Albert Einstein

"Either write something worth reading or do something worth writing."   Benjamin Franklin

CHAPTER 19

~Lee~1969-70—13-14 yrs. Old

"When will our consciences grow so tender that we will act to prevent human misery rather than to avenge it?"

Eleanor Roosevelt

If had had to pick the event of the decade, it would be watching space exploration go from an idea with Kennedy saying, "I believe that this nation should commit itself to achieving the goal, before the decade is out, of landing on the moon..." to actually seeing it achieved eight years later when Neil Armstrong said, "That's one small step for man; one giant leap for mankind," as he stepped down the ladder on to lunar soil. Our family, along with an estimated 650 million people, watched that first lunar landing July 20,

1969. I was thirteen years old. I am sad that it divided the races rather than brought them together in my community. I hope that the movie *Hidden Figures* helped all races see the part black women played in getting Americans to space despite the discrimination they faced and made the event more believable.

Putting a man on the moon wasn't the only memorable American event during the Summer of '69. Three other things happened besides going to the moon and being told I was skipping a grade. During the flight to the moon in July, Senator Edward Kennedy left a beach party on a resort island off Martha's Vineyard called Chappaquiddick and had an auto accident. He'd had too much to drink and plunged off a bridge into water, killing 28-year-old Mary Jo Kopechne. He survived, but his reputation did not. A couple of weeks later on August 8, five people were murdered in the home of actress Sharon Tate, who was eight months pregnant. Her death and her guests' as well as two more murders in the neighborhood were committed by Charles Manson in a bizarre drug-fueled cult he had formed. (Leave a light on to read about the Manson Murders in a detailed book by Vincent Bugliosi called Helter Skelter.) Then the summer ended with the mother of all concerts, 300,000 rock music fans descending on a farm in upstate New York for Woodstock. Noted performers were Janis Joplin, Jimi Hendrix (neither of whom would be around the next year), the Grateful Dead, Crosby, Steels, and Nash, Joan Baez, the Jefferson Airplane, and Creedance Clearwater.

When summer was over, I had to start Bishopville High. I felt like I did when I was in first grade all over again—I didn't fit in anywhere. Just as before, I didn't fit in with the kids from the city. It wasn't so apparent at the Academy. Now, I also didn't fit in the eighth grade or the ninth. I really didn't feel a part of either. I felt like I had been kicked out of the eighth and not accepted into the ninth, through no fault of my own. Also, I was a bookworm and had never been able to participate in sports and had no interest in things like cheerleading or band because of my severe allergies. Everyone else seemed to pick a sport, a band instrument, or become a cheerleader, while I went to the library to read or with older kids to art classes. The few friends I did have were also introverts not involved in other activities. They were city kids though, and I could not talk to them like I could Shine! I missed her so much; but even when she came home, it seemed as if she'd outgrown me and was angry with me and everyone around her.

Outside of our life at the farm, white people did not comingle with blacks. Adeline and I were too big to play in the woods and too bashful to invite the other into our homes (her because she was embarrassed and me because I didn't want my family to say anything out of the way like my mother did to Lizzie). Also, we were interested in boys and didn't make much time for each other anymore when she was in Bishopville. However, we did run into each other occasionally.

The next time I saw Adeline was the next summer when I ran out of gas. I got my permit to drive when I turned fourteen, but I don't ever remember not being able to drive. When you grow up on a farm, as soon as you can see over a steering wheel and your foot can reach a gas pedal, you are driving something, a riding lawn mower, then a tractor, a truck and a car. In this case, my mother had sent me up to the church to get something. In the 1960s the church as well as our house was always unlocked, unlike today. It was only a mile away, but she sent me in her car on an empty tank, more than likely to get large baking pans for cooking for the upcoming funeral. After I pulled over to the side of the road, I had only gotten a few steps passed the car to walk home when a car flew by me. Then the old car pulled into someone's driveway and turned around and headed straight for me. I thought it was going to run me over! It was Adeline!

"Oh, my goodness! It's you! You are home! What are you doing here?"

"I am picking up hitchhikers," Adeline said, "You want a ride?"

I hopped in. "Yeah. Thanks. Can you please take me to the farm to get some gas? I ran out. When did you get home! You look like a woman! Look at you!"

"And look at you, driving a car by yourself. Why'd you let it run out of gas, girl?"

"Aw, Adeline, you know how Mama is. You would think with a pump being at the farm, the gas tank would always be full."

"Yes, lawd, when I tell my friends up North y'all has your own gas pump, they don't believe me; but them tractors take a lot of fuel. Y'all don't exactly stay home either. Vern needs to put a pump in Miss Joannie's yard!" Adeline said, laughing. "Tell me what's going on, shug."

"Oh, the worst has happened, Adeline. You know my friend Randy Davis that went to Viet Nam on two tours of duty? Our whole community just adores him. We just got word that he got hit by shrapnel trying to save his buddies and was killed. We are all heartbroken," I started sniffling.

Adeline brought the car to a dead stop. She just sat there, breathing heavy.

"Adeline, are you ok? Did you know Randy?"

She just sat there for a minute as tears welled in her eyes, gritting her teeth.

"I knew him, kind of. My friend died, too. When is this nonsense gonna stop, Lee? When?"

I wasn't used to seeing Adeline cry so I knew this "friend" must have been important to her.

"Oh my, Adeline. I am so sorry you lost someone, too. Listen, we better get on down to the farm to get the gas and then I want you to tell me all about your friend and I will tell you about our Randy. He was the best, so funny, and the whole community loved him. When I have a son, I will be damned if he ever gets to play with guns, much less join the Army!"

"I know what you mean, child. Ain't nothing good coming from it. Nothing."

And then we sang the song "War" together. It came on the radio as if on cue. "War" was one of the most popular protest songs, produced first by the Temptations and then by Edwin Starr.

> War, huh, yeah
> What is it good for?
> Absolutely nothing, uhh
> War, huh, yeah
> What is it good for?
> Absolutely nothing
> Say it again, y'all
> War, huh (good God)
> What is it good for?
> Absolutely nothing, listen to me, oh

> War, I despise
> 'Cause, it means the destruction of innocent lives
> War means tears to thousands of mother's eyes
> When their sons go off to fight
> And lose their lives

> (repeat chorus)

> It ain't nothing but a heartbreaker
> War-Friend only to the Undertaker
> Oh, it's an enemy to all mankind
> The thought of war blows my mind
> War has caused unrest
> Within the younger generation
> Induction and then destruction
> Who wants to die? Oh

(repeat chorus)

It ain't nothing but a heartbreaker
War-it's got one friend, that's the Undertaker
Oh, war has shattered many a young man's dreams
Made him disabled, bitter, and mean
Life is too precious
To spend fighting wars each day
War can't give life
It can only take it away, oh

(repeat chorus)

It ain't nothing but a heartbreaker
War-Friend to the Undertaker-woo
Peace, love, and understanding, tell me
Is there no place for them today?
They say we must fight to keep our freedom
But Lord knows there's got to be a better way, oh

War, huh, God y'all
What is it good for? You tell me-nothing!
War, good God, huh, now huh

What is it good for?
Stand up and shout it: Nothing!
Say it, say it, say it

"Lee, girl, you still can't sing!"
"You neither!" I giggled. "So, tell me about your friend."
As we got the gas and made it back to the car to fill it, Adeline told me about losing the love of her life in the war and I told her about what a funny, brave young man our hometown hero Randy Davis was.

"So, what beings you home, Adeline?"

"I come to straighten out some business with my sisters. My dad died in March you know. Or maybe you didn't. He had been up North with us."

"Oh, no, Adeline. I am so sorry. I hadn't heard."

"Yep, at least the old codger lived long enough to see me finish school. And guess what? I am going to get my associates degree."

"Wow! I am so proud of you!" I said, hugging Adeline. "You've come a long way, baby."

"Yeah, I sure have. I have come a long, long way from these cotton fields. Maybe in another ten years I'll be sitting with you at a table in a restaurant without people staring at us and sitting on the bottom floor with you in the movie theater. Maybe somebody will write a book and document just how ridiculous black people were treated."

Adeline drove off into the sunset and I did not see or hear from her for another fifty years when we got together to write this book.

Colored Seated in the Rear

EPILOGUE
~*~*~*~

If you remember in the prologue, I called the county library and asked if any black women around my age frequented the library who may have grown up on our farm. I figured if they liked to read, they may be interested in writing also. I was so delighted to find that Adeline Reddick worked there. It was incredulous that she had moved back to South Carolina and lived surrounded by land that I owned and neither of us knew it. What was even more incredible was that she had been one of my playmates and co-workers on the farm! When Dawn Ellen, the librarian, said that Adeline was there, that was definitely a "God wink" this book should be written. And there were many more God winks to come.

Adeline and I immediately got together and started planning this project. If anyone had told us how much research and manhours and illnesses (including Covid-19) and how many hurdles and gut-wrenching emotions we would go through to get the book done, I am not sure either of us would have committed to it. However, once we started it, you all kept us going with your support and belief in us.

My previous project had been finishing my dad's extensive research on our family history. He did it with no computer before he died in 2006 while I had the luxury and ease of Ancestry.com. While getting reacquainted with Adeline, I told her about that project and mentioned that I found out that one of my eighth great-grandfather and several above him were Cherokee Indian chiefs. Adeline shared that she had Cherokee in her bloodline. We teased about perhaps being related since we certainly have many of the same personality traits. I asked if she wanted me to research her family history and of course, she said yes.

So, on top of writing the book and doing research on both of our families, I was driving back and forth between Florida and South Carolina every month or so, listening to Audible books during the eight-hour drive. Just by chance and a huge God wink, one of the books I heard was *Slavery by Another Name* by Douglas A. Blackmon. After listening to this book and doing Adeline's genealogy, I realized that Adeline's great grandfather, Joe Jackson, did not just abandon his family like her family had been told for three generations. The entire time I had known Adeline both growing up and while writing the book, she frequently griped about her great grandfather leaving her great grandmother, Minnie, to raise their five children to alone. I knew from Adeline that they were recruited from South Carolina to work in mines in Alabama owned by steel mills in Pennsylvania. Then when I listened to the book *Slavery by Another Name*, I suspected what happened to Joe Jackson was the same thing that happened to tens of thousands of strong young black men in the early 1900s that were taken to Alabama, many of which were never seen again.

According to the book, in the late 1800s and early 1900s, officials from the Birmingham coal and iron mines owned by US Steel would visit prisons in FL, GA, MS, AL, and SC to barter for prisoners to work for the mines, telling those states they would take care of the prisoners' expenses for six months or so, saving those states thousands of tax dollars. Often, they never brought the prisoners back. Some died of pneumonia, tuberculosis, and other diseases due to the poor, filthy conditions. Whipping bosses sometimes beat them to death. Also, human labor trafficking was rampant, sometimes picking up black men for made up charges such as loitering, flirting with white women, or ignoring "white only" or "colored seated in the rear" signs. Some, like Joe, had contracts and were promised a higher wage than in the state they resided just because they were strong and muscular, but often the mines would find a trumped-up charge to extend a legitimate contract.

I did some digging into Ancestry and into prison records and set out to prove what happened to Joe before telling Adeline. What I found was that Joe Jackson was indeed enticed to go to work in Alabama for a higher wage than he could make in South Carolina on a contract that he had to more or less work off like an indentured servant. His wife was allowed to come and cook for the camp because she was an excellent cook. Joe and Minnie of had a couple of children when they left and a few more during the years they were in Alabama, and. by all accounts, had an excellent marriage. However, unbeknownst to Minnie, Joe happened to be in the wrong place at the wrong time after work one day and never made it home to his family. He was falsely accused of something, arrested and put in jail under horrid conditions. Joe awaiting trial in prison and had no way of getting word to Minnie. He died in 1918 of the Spanish Flu while still in jail. Poor Miss Minnie and his children and most of his grandchildren never lived long enough to know what happened to him until over a century later when Adeline would hear this from me.

Oh, by the way, I never found any evidence that Adeline and I were blood related though her genealogy still needs much work. Regardless, we are still as close as any two sisters can be. One of her last birthdays, I gave her a Rosa Parks Barbie Doll.

"Oh, Lee, I can't believe it! I have never had one before!" Adeline exclaimed, wiping away tears as she opened her gift.

"Wow, is that the first Barbie you've ever had?" I asked, delighted I had given her something she seemed to really like.

"No, it's the first *doll* any one has ever given me."

ABOUT THE AUTHOR

Lee is the daughter of the late JoAnn and Laverne McCaskill of Bishopville, SC. She attended both public and private schools in Lee County and graduated from Clemson University in Microbiology with a minor in English. After several years as a research microbiologist and technical writer for USDA, she became an inventor, author, and entrepreneur, owning several businesses in Florida and South Carolina. Lee has co-authored many cookbooks and several books, including Wake Up and Live the Life you Love: Living in Clarity and Belly Bustin' Tips you can use on ANY Diet. She currently resides on Hutchinson Island in Fort Pierce, Florida.

ABOUT THE CONTRIBUTOR

Adeline is the daughter of the late Colin and Ruth Jackson Reddick of Bishopville, SC, and currently resides in the Turkey Creek section of Lee County. She went to Lee County Public Schools until she was sixteen and then to Sexton Jr. High in Camden, NJ, and finishing in Washington, DC. She worked in the DC public schools as a school bus attendant for handicapped children, and also at Georgetown Preparatory School (where Ethel Kennedy sent some of her children) preparing lunch. She also has her CNA license and has worked as an assistant in the Lee County Public Library. Adeline has entertained with her many stories, but this is her first published story.